The
Essential
Carer's
Guide

The Essential Carer's Guide

Mary Jordan

Foreword by
Philip Wroughton
Vice President,
Princess Royal Trust for Carers

Hammersmith Press
London, UK

First published in 2006 by Hammersmith Press Limited,
496 Fulham Palace Road, London SW6 6JD, UK

© Mary Jordan 2006

British Library Cataloguing in Publication Data: a CIP record for
this book is available from the British Library.

ISBN 1-905140-07-X

Designed by Julie Bennett
Production by Helen Whitehorn, Pathmedia
Printed and bound by MPG Books Ltd, UK
Cover image: Jo Knowles

Contents

Acknowledgements

Although I have written from the starting point of my own experience, I have had to do considerable research and I have been helped by many people. I would specifically like to mention and thank the following: Professor Basant K Puri MA (Cantab), PhD, MB, BChir, BSc (Hons) MathSci, MRCPsych, DipStat, MMath for his advice on The Mental Health Act and his valuable comments about Nutrition in the elderly; Dr Helen McGinty MB ChB, MRCGP, for editing the chapter on medical matters; Sharon Boylett MSc, PGdip, NDN, DipN, RGN for the information she gave about the service provided by District Nurses; Seamus Mahon for advice on nursing and care homes; and Mick Hanneghan for information about social services.

The case stories in this book have come from many sources and I wish to thank Patricia Palmer, Peter Palmer, Sara Clayton, Joan Zilva and Liz Jones specifically. Some who have passed on their own experiences have asked to remain anonymous but I give them my thanks for their contributions.

For the photographs in Chapter 5, I would like to thank *Keep Able* (www.keepable.co.uk) for permission to reproduce them from their latest catalogue and for supplying good quality originals.

I would not have been able to complete the book at all without the support of my husband, Chris, and my two sons and my daughter-in-law who 'kept me going when the world got tough'.

Foreword

Life offers many opportunities and challenges and assuming a caring role has to be one of the greatest challenges anyone can face in their lives. Suddenly nothing is the same as it was and you have to confront the prospect of changing your plans and ambitions. The estimated six million carers in the UK today have had to accept that position.

When someone becomes a carer they do not necessarily realise what the long term effects will be. Their relationship with the person for whom they care will almost certainly change. They may have to give up work and see their friends less often. They will experience the physical and emotional strain of round the clock caring. Many do not realise that support is available with the consequence that they reach breaking point before requesting help.

Mary Jordan has created a valuable guide to carers with practical information and quotes from carers whereby readers will realise they are not alone. Caring can also be a very enriching experience and I hope this handbook will help many people manage their caring responsibilities in a positive manner.

Philip Wroughton
Vice President
The Princess Royal Trust for Carers

Introduction

The idea for this book came from my personal experience of acting as a carer. Once I started talking about my experiences and the problems I was encountering I began to realise that there are many, many carers out there. Everyone who is a carer wants to do their best for the one they are caring for and everyone seems to have a story to tell about their experiences. I received a lot of support from others in my period as a carer and exchanged much helpful information. Of course I thought it would be useful if the information I collected and the experience I gained could be pulled together in one place, but it also seemed to me that a book like this could be more than a collection of facts. So I have included case stories wherever I have thought them relevant.

All the stories in this book are true stories, although sometimes the relationships have been changed to protect identities. In this way I hope that, in reading this book, you will gain something of the experience of belonging to a support group - in other words, the feeling that you are not alone and that you can gain from reading someone else's solutions to their problems.

I also wanted to make this book a resource tool – a start on the research path to find help and support. So I have included 'Further Information' which refer to particular chapter subject matter as well as a global 'Useful contacts' section at the end of a book.

My thoughts about how this book might be used have influenced its layout. You may be looking for advice or information about just one area of caring; alternatively, you may want to read up on the whole subject. So I have included individual chapter references which refer to the particular chapter subject matter as well as a global 'Useful contacts' section at the end of the book. There are inevitably some repetitions but I hope this makes the book more helpful rather than otherwise.

Some terminology has proved difficult. I am aware that some of us are caring for neighbours or friends rather than relatives. I have therefore opted for the generalised expression, favoured by many of the Carers' charities and support groups, 'the Cared-for'. If you can think of a better, I will consider it for the second edition.

I also know that not all carers are caring for the elderly but there was a need to set some parameters to a book on such a vast subject. Much of the information in this book will be relevant to you if you are caring for a younger person, whether a relative or not, but the emphasis is on the increasing physical and mental frailty of old age.

There is an enormous amount of information here, yet I know it is not comprehensive. If there is something important you think should be added please write to me c/o Hammersmith Press (www.hammersmithpress.co.uk).

1

Managing change

My mother had a lot of trouble getting up from the sitting position due to a bad hip. It would take her ages to get up out of her chair if the doorbell rang or if she needed something from the next room. I could see that a 'riser/recliner' chair would be a real boon to her but she refused to buy one even though she could afford it. In the end the family clubbed together and bought it as a birthday gift. Even then she resisted putting it in the sitting room where her usual chair was placed. Eventually, we installed the chair and showed her how to use it. At first she wouldn't use the mechanism, insisting on dragging herself up as before. Finally, my brother got quite cross with her and insisted that she use it. Within a week she was proclaiming to all and sundry what a marvellous invention it was!

Changes are hard for many of us and one of the biggest difficulties you may encounter whilst acting as carer may be trying to get your elderly relative or friend to change anything – routines, furniture, habitation – with which they are familiar. Even those who do not suffer from dementia may resist change. It takes some elderly people longer than others to come to terms with a new idea. An elderly person in the early stage of dementia may actually find any change in routine quite frightening.

This means it is important first to decide whether a change is really necessary. Often it can appear that a new way of doing things, a new piece of equipment, a move to new living accommodation, or an alteration in routine would be of benefit to our Cared-for and we take it for granted that they will feel the same way about it. However, elderly people need familiar things and faces around them and may regard new people in their life, new items of furniture and especially new routines with suspicion. Even when something new would make life easier for them they may resist. It is easy to become very impatient with this type of resistance. If you want to introduce any change consider it in three steps:

- Is the change actually necessary or just convenient?
- Can smaller alterations or adjustments be made to prevent the need (or put off the need) for a major change?
- How can any necessary change be introduced in the least challenging way?

Moving home

Necessary or just convenient?

It often seems obvious to carers that the home of their Cared-for is inconvenient and difficult to manage for someone less mobile than they used to be (and perhaps even a bit infirm). The inclination is to suggest a move – to a bungalow, a smaller house, or a warden managed complex, or a Care home. It may be hard to understand the outright resistance such a suggestion often provokes. But it is the very familiarity of the living space which provides reassurance to the elderly person. The home is familiar to them; they automatically know where every hand-hold is as they move from room to room. Their belongings are all stowed in familiar places so that they need scarcely think to carry out their everyday tasks. They may already have made small adaptations – moving a rug so that it doesn't cause them to trip, using an extension cord to make a power point easier to reach, adding a lower shelf in the bathroom – in the past to make their environment more convenient. Many elderly people have also gone to great lengths to make their home secure, installing door and window locks, for example, or a door chain and they feel secure and relaxed indoors and in their own garden. Naturally they are resistant to the very idea of leaving these familiar surroundings. All this is quite apart from the simple fact that a widow or widower may have many happy memories of times spent with their partner in the house or flat where they may have lived together for many years. To move may seem like leaving the partner behind, even more than the loss due to death.

It is well documented that many elderly people who are forced to move home go from being quite self-sufficient and managing well around the house to needing help and being unable to cope. In part this is due to the unfamiliarity of the new home and to the loss of the sense of security which the elderly person previously had.

Can small adjustments prevent major change?

First, examine the present environment. Through social services or through the district nursing team you can ask for and arrange an occupational therapy (OT) assessment of your Cared-for's home to plan where small adjustments can make the environment safer and more comfortable. The therapists will advise about such things as ramps to outside doors, grab rails, raised toilet seats, non-slip rugs, bathing aids and so forth. Usually your Cared-for or the immediate family will be expected to make the actual arrangements for these changes and to pay for them, although some items (raised toilet seats, for example) can be given on loan. The OT assessors will produce a written plan for any changes and agree with your Cared-for (and you if you are present) on how the changes might be implemented and who is responsible for the implementation. If your Cared-for has suffered an illness or accident and spent some time in hospital, then they will not normally be sent home from hospital until an assessment of the home environment has been conducted to see if they can manage alone at home.

After Mum died we were appalled to discover the extent to which Dad was unable to manage. Mum had been helping him so much that we had not realized how difficult he found it to get up and down from a chair, to pull plugs out of the wall sockets and even to do things like opening food cans. My sister and I thought that a care home was the only answer but the GP arranged an OT assessment of the house for us. The OT assessor showed us how a number of quite minor things like an electric can opener, some special grips for the taps and electric plugs could make a huge difference. Of course Dad wanted to carry on living at home as long as he could, so luckily he made a big effort to learn to use all the 'aids'.

Some simple changes such as those mentioned above may make your Cared-for's life at home safer and more convenient for them. It may also give you, the carer, a little more peace of mind. From a safety point of view, a number of small changes can make the home more secure. Good door locks and a chain and a spy-hole are the first essentials, though the chain should be used only to answer the door, not left on in case you, the carer, needs to gain entrance in an emergency. Your Cared-for should be persuaded always to use the door chain if they do not know who the caller is. It is worth making a point that they should not let anyone into the house unless they are known to them. Bona fide traders will carry identification but this is possible to imitate. An easily purchased and fitted closed circuit TV camera by the front door may give you and your Cared-for some peace of mind. These are obtainable from DIY stores and can be attached to the normal television for viewing who is at the door. They take only a few moments to fit and this can be done by anyone reasonably competent at DIY.

Introducing necessary major changes in the least challenging way

If a house move is really vital then you will need to approach things slowly. This is something for the whole family to discuss and consider. Strangely what often happens is that all the family talk around a solution and forget to include the elderly relative or friend in question in their discussions! Remember that it is the elderly person and their needs which are being discussed as well as the convenience of the carers. You should ask your Cared-for what their preferences are. They may be adamant that they want to stay in their own house. It will take time and patience to convince them otherwise. It may help to take all the alternatives and discuss them one by one, pointing out the pros and cons and explaining the possibilities.

- Moving in with family or friends – consider the following: is there room available in the home of any of the family? Are the family prepared to make any changes necessary in their household? How would privacy issues be managed? What financial contribution would your relative or friend make to the household? What would be the effect on other members of the household?

- Living alone – consider the following: can a suitable house, bungalow or flat be found near to one or other family member so that visitors can drop in and perhaps grandchildren be taken to visit? Does your Cared-for need to have help on hand in case of emergency (warden managed accommodation)? Can help be arranged for tasks which are too difficult (professional carers or family members and friends)?
- Moving to a communal residential home – Few elderly people look forward to the idea of giving up their independence in this way. It will take time and much discussion to persuade your elderly relative or friend that this is the right move. Consider what type of accommodation is necessary? How much can your Cared-for afford in fees? In what area should you look for a home? (For further useful discussion see Chapter 11 on Care/Nursing homes)

Getting out and about

If your elderly Cared-for has always been driven or accompanied by their partner they may resist the very idea of taking buses or taxis and expect you or some other member of their family to carry out the job of chauffeur and companion as their partner did. You may be prepared to do this, but it will still involve some changes in their routine.

Can small adjustments prevent major change?

Can your relative or friend drive themselves? You may only need to help them to gain confidence in going out alone. Otherwise, you may need to give some very active help in the way of applying for bus passes, writing down taxi service telephone numbers and initially accompanying them on the bus or in the taxi until they are familiar with these new modes of travel.

Introducing the change in the least challenging way

Try to give full attention to the details which may make your Cared-for reluctant to use these services. For example, they may not like waiting at bus stops alone because they are afraid of being attacked and 'mugged'. They may feel awkward getting in and out of taxis if they are a little disabled or they may feel that they do not know how much to tip the taxi driver. If driving your Cared-for around regularly is likely to cause you severe inconvenience, then it is worth persevering in trying to overcome these objections. You might, for example, suggest that your Cared-for teams up with a neighbour for trips on the bus. You might investigate whether there is a local taxi service which specializes in helping the elderly. (See Chapter 4 on Getting about.)

You may consider that your Cared-for would be helped by using a walking aid long before they accept the idea. Use of a simple walking stick may not be resisted much, but to many the notion of using a 'zimmer frame' is totally unacceptable. Fortunately there are many modern wheeled walking aids available now which may be found more acceptable (see Chapter 4). Your Cared-for should be the one who chooses the walking aid and there are many shops and mobility centres where you can take them to try out different styles and designs. Ask the District Nurse where would be the best place for you to go locally to look at walking aids. The District Nurse may suggest that your elderly relative, or friend, has a physiotherapy assessment to decide the most suitable frame or trolley. It may help to persuade a reluctant user if it is suggested that it can at first just be used 'now and again'. Once used to the mobility and stability which these aids give, most users are enthusiasts and recommend them to friends.

New furniture and fittings

Necessary or just convenient?

Buying new furniture to replace that which has grown shabby is just convenient. Replacing items which are damaged and might cause accidents (electric fires, cookers, worn rugs etc) is necessary. A newer and better washing machine might just be convenient. A microwave might be necessary. The most difficult step will probably be to persuade your Cared-for to accept the new items, but people differ in this as in everything else.

After my mother had her stroke she was so keen not to be a burden that she immediately asked me to order her meals-on-wheels and to arrange the purchase of a walker trolley so that she would be allowed home. My mother-in-law on the other hand refused even to accept a helping hand to get in and out of the car and could never be brought to see that in refusing help of any kind she placed more of a burden on all of us.

Can small adjustments prevent major change?

Consider whether clearer instructions would help someone use the equipment they already own more easily. User instructions can be scanned into a computer and reprinted in larger print, for example. Could moving the furniture or equipment make it easier to use? Perhaps an extension cord would facilitate this. Would a larger kitchen bin mean fewer trips out to the dustbin? Would moving some existing table lamps save moving a favourite chair into a different position? Would a grab rail mean there was no need for a raised toilet seat?

Introducing the change in the least challenging way

Remember that it is not you who is going to use the furniture or the equipment every day; it is your elderly relative, or friend. Discuss with them whether a particular appliance or piece of equipment would make their life easier. Expect reluctance to agree on their part and take the time to talk through the reasons why a particular item might help, stressing that it will help them to remain independent. Many people are converted to an idea after they have seen how it makes life easier for a friend or neighbour, so if you can show them say, the way that 'old Mrs so-and-so down the road gets about with her walker trolley' it might be a real advantage. You could collect a few catalogues and take time to look through them to see which particular type of equipment might be most useful. Disablity Centres and shops welcome visitors and here you will be able to touch and try out different equipment or to see it demonstrated.

Once your Cared-for is in possession of the appliance or piece of equipment make sure that they know how to use it. For major items such as a stairlift, the suppliers will often include a familiarization session as part of the supply package but you may still need to ensure that your Cared-for uses the equipment on a daily basis and does not forget instructions for use. For some items (a rising/reclining chair with an electric motor, for example) you may find that you need to go over the methods of use several times before your Cared-for is confident in their use.

If you are arranging for a new appliance (such as a microwave oven) which your elderly Cared-for may not be familiar with, then you will need to take some time to demonstrate how it can be used and to stress safety measures for use. If a family member is competent on a computer they can scan direction leaflets and print them out in large print. Alternatively, you might reduce the instructions to their most basic and copy these out and leave in a prominent place near the equipment. As an example, if your elderly Cared-for acquires an automatic washing machine and will only be likely to use one or two programmes, write out clearly the instructions for these and tape them to the machine.

None of the above is meant to imply that your Cared-for is too stupid to understand instructions. Indeed, many elderly people will take a delight in learning to use all the functions of a piece of equipment and get full use from it. Others with perhaps poor sight or poor concentration will find the above measures make life easier for them.

Help in the house

Necessary or just convenient?

Can your Cared-for manage all that is necessary even if it takes them a little longer than it might take you? Can you or another family member undertake to do what they can't manage without too much inconvenience or difficulty?

Can small adjustments prevent major change?

Small adjustments can range from a little occasional part-time help with difficult jobs such a gardening or window cleaning to visits on a regular basis for set jobs. Elderly people are often quite amenable to having someone help with the 'heavy' cleaning and if it is a simple cleaning service that is needed, this is best obtained by advertising locally or using a cleaning agency. The agencies are much more expensive but you and your Cared-for have the benefit of knowing that the cleaning staff have had their references checked and have a reputation to maintain with the agency. It may not be very difficult to persuade your relative, or friend, that they need extra help in the house but some people feel that having 'a stranger' coming into the house is an invasion of their privacy. They may try to convince you that they can manage by themselves or may ask you to help them instead. A lot of gentle persuasion may be needed. It might help to go through tasks with your Cared-for and try to start in a small way. Perhaps someone could come in just to trim the hedges to start with, or just to clean the windows once a month. This 'toe in the water' approach may then make your Cared-for more amenable to extend the help. On the other hand, you may have to be quite firm in pointing out that your own time is limited if this is the case and that your Cared-for will have to begin to trust others for some of these tasks. Unless your Cared-for is on a very low income there is unlikely to be any free help available and it may be that you and they will have to settle for the amount of help they can afford.

It is quite important when organizing help in the house to go through the tasks which you and your Cared-for require to be done and to specify how frequently. You may be surprised to discover that some cleaners 'don't do beds' or that others consider cleaning and defrosting the fridge to be outside of their duties, for example. If you are considering using an agency, then it helps to make careful enquiries in the first telephone call. Some specify that they only handle 'light housework' which is the area your Cared-for can probably manage themselves. It is the heavier work where help is most often needed such as vacuuming under beds, cleaning windows and ovens, mowing the lawn. Other help agencies specialize in offering companionship, running small errands and doing light shopping but do not offer cleaning services at all. Make a list of the tasks that need doing. Make a shortlist of likely agencies or private cleaners. Then telephone each and ask first if they or their staff will undertake these tasks before entering into enquiries about prices or availability. This will save a good deal of time in the long run.

My mother and father had had the services of a cleaner once a week for a few years. Gradually on my visits I began to notice that some things were not as clean as they could be and that the bedclothes were changed very infrequently. I asked them why the cleaner wasn't doing the work but they always prevaricated. Eventually I asked the cleaner directly. She told me then that she 'didn't do beds or bathrooms' and that this had been understood by my parents when they employed her. But of course, as they grew more frail, they were unable to do these things themselves. They liked the woman and did not want to upset her or lose her services. In the end the solution was to employ a second cleaner to do the things the first one wouldn't do!

Introducing the change in the least challenging way

Accepting help with personal care is one of the biggest challenges that may face your Cared-for. Many people need help as they grow older with dressing, washing and toileting due to disability from arthritis or other disabling conditions and people with dementia need help in these areas because they become unable to begin or to carry through simple everyday personal care. Most of us very much dislike the idea of having help with personal care and your elderly relative, or friend, may disguise their need for such help as long as they can. Some people will insist that they need help from you, especially if you are a relative, and not from an outsider even when they know you are unable to provide it due to other commitments.

My mother needed help to get in and out of bed after her stroke. She also needed some help with fastenings and things like that when dressing. However, she was quite capable of managing to use the toilet and of washing and showering herself. For ages she refused to tell us that she needed any help because she was terrified that any carer would insist on helping her to wash or shower. Once we discovered what worried her we were able to arrange for a carer to come in the morning and evening but gave them strict instruction to let Mum wash herself and use the toilet in privacy. For the first week one of us visited when the carer came to ensure that our instructions were carried out. This gave Mum confidence and she accepted the help she needed.

On the other hand some people would prefer to accept such help from professionals rather than from a relative or friend. It might help to point out that those who provide personal care choose to do it because they like helping others, that they are specially trained, that they are used to the tasks which your Cared-for might find embarrassing. It will certainly help if you allow your Cared-for to get used to the idea gradually, to help in selecting the provider and to give a clear idea of what help they want and need and what they can manage for themselves. Here again there are many items of equipment available to help those with minor disabilities remain independent for as long as possible (see Chapter 5 on OT aids and equipment.)

Summing up

Managing change will be more successful if you apply the above simple principles. Change management entails thoughtful planning and sensitive implementation, and above all, consultation with, and involvement of, the people affected by the changes. If you force change on people, especially elderly people, difficult problems can arise.

In all cases of necessary change, be prepared to be patient, to involve your Cared-for in decisions and to allow them to talk to voice their fears and worries beforehand. Where someone suffers from dementia or where not making the changes would endanger the safety of your Cared-for it may be necessary to be firm and even to over-rule them but where at all possible it will pay to introduce changes slowly and cautiously.

Further information – managing change

Cruse Bereavement Care
Help, counselling and support for the bereaved
www.crusebereavementwcare.org.uk
Helpline: 0870 167 1677

Disabled Living Foundation
Provides information and advice on equipment. There is an Equipment Demonstration Centre with large displays of items which visitors can try out and where advice can be obtained.
Helpline – 0845 130 9177 (charged at Local Call Rate
Equipment Demonstration Centre – (020) 7289 6111 ext.247
www.dlf.org.uk

Assist UK Disabled Living Centres
A network of centres around the UK, which provide information and advice on products and where you can see and try these out.
Tel: 0870 770 2866
www.dlcc.org.uk

Stair-lifts

Stannah
Tel: 0800 715 171
www.stannah.com

Brooks stairlifts
Tel: 0800 834730
www.stairlifts.co.uk

Walking Aids

Uniscan Walkers
Tel: 0800 0640762
www.uniscan-walkers.co.uk

Able Mail Order
Tel:0800 358 0445
www.independentliving.co.uk/able/mailorder.html

Accomodation

The Elderly Accommodation Counsel
for lists of homes in most areas
www.eac.org.uk
Tel:0207 820 1343

The Registered Nursing Home Association
for a list of registered nursing homes
www.rnha.co.uk
Tel: 0121 454 2511

BUPA Care homes
For a list of general things to look for when choosing a home
www.bupacarehomes.co.uk
Tel: 0800-00-10-10

2

After a bereavement

Service utilities and financial issues

My mother had become more and more frail in the two years before my father died. To be honest we all thought that she would be the first to go. Then my father died very suddenly after a short illness and we realised the extent of Mother's need for help in many areas of her life. I realised that I had become her chief carer. What took me aback was how many small everyday things I had to sort out so soon after his death – even things like re-arranging the electricity and gas bills. She just wasn't up to it.

This chapter focuses on what needs to be done when an elderly person loses their partner, generally through bereavement, though much of the information below is also relevant if their partner has to move into institutional care and can no longer remain with them at home.

When someone dies there are many things that have to be tackled immediately after and in connection with the death – things like registration of the death, administering the will and arranging the funeral. But there may also be multiple small practical considerations which need to be addressed simply to enable the surviving member of a partnership to continue their everyday life. It often falls to the carer to deal with these issues. There are likely to be many changes needed to documentation and some practical changes as well to help the surviving partner manage alone.

Changes to documentation

Any accounts/agreements in joint names will need to be changed to the name of the surviving account holder. There may be many more of these than are at first apparent. One way to find out is to go back through the bank statements and note all automatic payments out. This should reveal most commitments such as Council tax, rental agreements, insurances and membership fees. Remember that some direct debits and standing orders are only paid annually so check at least a year's worth of statements.

A simple method is to write two lists, one for those items where the account name needs to be changed and one for items needing cancellation. Most organisations will accept simple changes of name via the telephone but unless you hold Power of Attorney most will want to speak to the remaining account holder rather than a third party. If your Cared-for is unable to make the whole call most organisations will accept their verification of name and account details and their verbal permission to allow you to do the rest.

The good news is that most organisations are trained to react quickly and sympathetically to the report of a bereavement and many have a dedicated bereavement team to deal with changes to account names and any rebates or reductions in payments.

The not so good news is that many organisations have call centres to which any call is automatically routed and call centre staff are trained to respond in an automatic way. A good tip is to avoid answering any routine security questions and state immediately that you wish to report a death.

Don't allow this:

'Hello this is General Bank Plc, Robin speaking. Can I have your sort code please?"

'Er yes – it's 61-75-94'

'And your account number please'

'52305769'

'Account in the name of Charles and Vera Johnson. Can you give me your pass code please?'

'Er- no I haven't got that I........'

'I'm afraid I'll have to ask you some security questions then. What is your mother's maiden name?'

Instead:

'Hello this is General Bank Plc, Robin speaking. Can I have your sort code please?"

'Good morning. My name is Valerie Johnson and I wish to record the death of my father-in-law, Charles Johnson. Would you put me through to the correct department please.'

'Certainly. One moment please.'

Many organisations will require a copy of the death certificate (not a photocopy). When registering a death it is worth getting several copies of the death certificate at the time. The registrar will give you as many as you need but there is a small payment for each one. However, the payment is higher if you have to ask for extra copies later.

1. State pensions and council tax

When a death is registered the Registrar will normally ask for details of any pensions that are being administered by the State or by any public organisation such as the Armed Forces or the Civil Service. If possible, remember to take details of these pensions with you when you register the death. The Registrar will then inform the pension administrators of the death. Within a short time (days rather than weeks) the pension organisation will contact the widow/widower to follow up. If there is a widow's pension payable there will probably be some forms to complete but because the notification has come via the Registrar you may not need to forward a death certificate.

Many Registrars will also inform the local council of the death. One person living alone is eligible for a lower rate of council tax and a rebate of any overpayment previously made. Most councils will arrange this immediately they are informed of the death but if the widow or widower does not receive notification within a few weeks the matter should be followed up with the council concerned. If council tax is being paid by direct debit any rebate or adjustment will be made directly into the bank account from which the payment is made. Again you are unlikely to be asked for the death certificate in this case. Remember to check bank statements after the due date of the next payment to make sure your instructions have been acted upon.

2. Insurances

All insurance companies have dedicated bereavement teams who normally deal with any claims or administrative changes quickly. Life insurance companies will require an original copy of the death certificate but many property insurance companies do not, and will change the account details if you telephone them to explain. Be careful to ensure that you notify the company of all policies held and do not rely on their systems to work in your favour.

> I notified the insurance company of my mother's death and they dealt with the notification and the claim quickly and efficiently. However a couple of months later, when I was going through some of my mother's papers I discovered a second 'live' policy with the same company. Although they dealt with the second claim just as competently I felt that this smacked of 'sharp practice'. I am sure their computer systems must have shown that there was more than one policy in my mother's name and that they deliberately avoided telling me about it.

Car insurance may have to be completely re-assessed and a new policy issued depending upon whether the deceased or the remaining partner was the main insured driver.

3. Banks and building societies

Financial organisations generally have robust procedures for dealing with bereavement. They will need to see an original copy of the death certificate. It may be useful go into the branch of the organisation concerned rather than try to write or telephone. The clerk at the branch will then photocopy the death certificate, certify it as a true copy and return it to you. You can also usually complete any forms required on the spot. A joint account can usually be altered to continue in one name only with the minimum of trouble. However, it may be the case that only one partner (often the man) held the account in his name and dealt with all the finances. If this is the case, a new bank or building society account will need to be set up and each bank has its own regulations concerning this. You will need to enquire about these. At this stage, consider whether to set up a joint account with your Cared-for or whether to organise an Enduring Power of Attorney (see Chapter 3 on Financial matters). It may save you a lot of trouble later if you think about this now. Any debit cards on the account will probably need to be re-issued. If the bank forgets to mention this make sure that you ask them about it.

4. Credit cards

Credit card companies also have standard procedures for dealing with bereavement. Cards held in the sole name of the remaining partner will not be affected. However, where the remaining partner was only a secondary cardholder with a credit card company the account is not automatically changed to their name. The company will cancel the card and the remaining partner will have to re-apply in their own right for a card if this is required. Nor, as a general rule do card companies transfer a balance from the card of the deceased partner to the remaining partner. Any balances on credit cards are considered to be a debt on the estate and are due for payment, though interest is frozen on death. However, some credit card companies adopt a compassionate approach and actually cancel a debt on the death of the cardholder. You will need to ascertain the exact position with the individual company.

5. Rental agreements and utility bills

Ongoing rental agreements for items such as satellite television and telephones can usually be switched to the name of the remaining partner. Often the companies do not even require a copy of the death certificate and will make the switch once you confirm the details over the telephone, provided the payments continue to be made from the same bank account as before. The same applies to utility bills. Items no longer required (for example car breakdown insurance if the remaining partner does not drive and intends to sell the car) may need to be cancelled in writing. If such an agreement is annually renewed, a rebate for the unused portion of the agreement should be issued to the estate.

If the remaining partner is now in a straitened financial situation this would be the right time to investigate help with paying for utilities. There are national, local and charitable grants available to help people with low incomes in these circumstances (see Benefits on page 45.)

Practical matters concerning everyday living

Even if completely physically fit and mentally capable, your Cared-for may have problems dealing with some everyday tasks. Elderly people have often over the years developed their partnership so that only one of them carries out certain tasks. It is not uncommon, for example, to find that elderly men have no notion of cookery. Similarly, elderly women were born into a generation where it was common for only the man to be the car driver or to manage the finances.

My father always operated the video player and when he died my mother had no idea how to work it. She was also partially sight ed, which meant that she had difficulty in reading the instruction book or seeing the control buttons. Eventually we bought her a DVD player, which was much simpler to operate and because the instructions appear on the screen she was able to see them and to learn to operate it.

It may be up to you as the carer to assess the gaps in capabilities, and of course it may require tact and diplomacy both to discover and to address these gaps.

Lack of practical skills can be overcome in a number of ways. If your elderly relative or friend is amenable to learning a new skill this helps, but sometimes you may encounter resistance. On the other hand, many elderly people actually seem to gain a new lease of life after overcoming the initial shock of the death of a partner. They discover untapped depths within themselves. In this case there are many resources open to them. Local authorities offer (for example) classes in simple cookery, car maintenance, or simple house maintenance, and most of these classes positively welcome older people. Senior citizens usually receive a discount on the price of classes and, as an added extra, may make new acquaintances whilst attending them. You can research such classes either on the web or via your local library. The library and the internet are in nearly all cases invaluable sources of local information.

Sometimes your Cared-for may not want to learn a skill but may be quite amenable to making changes to get around the lack of it. For example, an elderly person may not want or be able to learn to cook. There are several alternatives to them cooking for themselves. Or they may not want to be bothered or may be unable to learn the ins and outs of how the bank accounts and bill paying work. There are ways of helping with this.

1. Meals and cooking

Meals-on-wheels

The meals-on-wheels (it may have another name depending on the area) scheme is operated by the local authority (LA) and you will need to contact them to find out what is available. Most LAs specify that the service is only available to those who are unable to cook a meal themselves but each has its own criteria to decide this. Your Cared-for will possibly have to be assessed by social services against the LA criteria. Some LAs will not supply meals if there is a carer available to do so. Some will offer cooked meals only; others will supply cook/chill meals, which can be re-heated or micro-waved; some will offer a choice or a mixture of both. Mostly these meals are delivered only once a day in the middle of the day and other arrangements will have to be made for breakfast and evening meals. The meals-on-wheels service is not free and will have to be paid for. It is normally a flat rate charge, usually below the cost of buying a hot meal elsewhere.

Ready meals

For someone who is able to operate a cooker or a microwave but who does not want to be bothered with cooking from scratch, there are a whole range of frozen and cook/chill meals available in every supermarket. The meals range from simple 'boil in the bag' items such as rice or microwaveable bags of fresh vegetables to complete 'roast dinners'. Most of them are very appetising and nutritionally adequate. Your Cared-for will probably need a freezer if they use this option unless shopping can be arranged several times each week.

Caring agencies

Most agency carers are happy to prepare a meal and serve it up but the amount of preparation time for a meal produced from fresh ingredients may make this an expensive option as agencies usually operate hourly charges (see Chapter 10 on Professional carers).

Neighbours and friends

Friends or neighbours who are at home during the day may be prepared to cook an extra portion when they cook for themselves and to carry it round to your Cared-for. This may not be a perfect answer because you would have to be sure that your friend/ neighbour would be prepared to do this on a regular basis. You would also have to be prepared to make other arrangements to cover times when they were on holiday or out for the day. However, it is certainly a solution worth investigating, especially as a stop gap.

2. Financial solutions

Joint accounts

If your Cared-for is happy to trust you in financial matters, and you are happy to help in this area, a good solution is to set up a joint bank account so that you can deal with bill payment, check that deposits from pensions etc. are being made and keep an eye on things generally. The bank branch where your Cared-for's account is held will be able to help with this.

Power of Attorney

You or your Cared-for may wish to consider Power of Attorney as an option. If your Cared-for sets up a Power of Attorney naming you as the attorney you will then have the power to manage all their financial affairs for them. There are many factors to consider and it is best to consult a solicitor, but you can get information from The Public Guardianship Office. One thing you must be aware of is that only *Enduring* Power of Attorney will give you control that will continue should your Cared-for becomes mentally incapable; Ordinary Power of Attorney will not give you this option (see Further information on page 34 and Chapter 3 on Financial matters).

Direct debits

Many utilities and rental firms will happily organise direct debit or standing order payments for their services and this may work very well. Bills are sent out as before but the amount required to pay the bill is collected via a direct debit. This needs to be set up with each individual utility or rental company, but is a very good way of ensuring regular payment especially if, as sometimes happens, your Cared-for 'forgets' or 'loses' mail.

> My mother-in-law couldn't cope with the bill paying etc. but wanted to feel that she was in control. We set up direct debit payments for electricity, gas and telephone and this meant that there were never any 'red' bills but at the same time she felt that she knew what was going on.

3. Gardening and house maintenance

If your Cared-for is unable to cope with simple things like mowing the lawn or changing light bulbs it probably means that either you, as the carer, or friends and neighbours, will have to help out. For more complicated tasks such as hedge cutting, plumbing and electrical problems you will need to call on outside help and this will usually have to be paid for. Indeed, paying for regular help in the garden or for large but irregular tasks such as decorating the house is a good solution provided your Cared-for can afford this. However (and particularly if the financial situation is difficult), there are alternatives.

Social services and local authorities

Social services do not usually provide this type of help but they may have information as to what is available locally. Local authorities may run schemes to help with house maintenance or house alterations to make life easier for frail elderly people.

Local charities

Local schemes are often in place to help elderly or disabled people. The local Lions club, Rotaract (the 'action' branch of the Rotary Club) and local Scout Groups are likely sources of help. It is not always easy to find information about what help these groups might offer but the best starting point to find a contact for such groups is your local library.

Churches and clubs

If the person you care for is or was a regular churchgoer, approach their church via the priest or minister. Even where there is no regular helping scheme in place, for such things church congregations will often rally to help someone in need. Similarly, if your Cared-for was a regular member of a local social club it may be worth approaching their members to ask for help. There may be a keen gardener or DIY expert who will be happy to help.

Making changes

Some elderly people may just be resistant to new or different things. They are capable of independent thought and action but just seem to be stubborn and unable to change. In such cases you sometimes have to insist. They may understand 'I want to help but I really can't manage every day' or 'We are not well ourselves and cannot do these things' or 'Let me help you set this up and then you will have control,' but equally they may not. For your own sanity you may just have to over-rule them. It isn't the best way but it may be the only way. Certainly, if you can arrange that the whole family is in agreement on any approach to change it will make implementing necessary alterations much easier. Family, or group, meetings and agreement are vital at this point.

> My mother-in-law would not accept any help in the house. Then my husband suffered a stroke. I simply said ' You are having this outside help because your son is ill and he and I cannot cope at this moment without this extra help'. She accepted it very grudgingly as an interim thing but the door had been opened and everything was easier afterwards.

4. General health

This is a good time to ensure co-ordination of health provision. Your Cared-for may see the family GP regularly and possibly the district nursing service will have been in contact. But if they and their former partner were in generally good health they may not have seen their doctor for months or even years. GPs in the NHS may have up to 3000 patients on their list and it is very easy to slip through any safety net there is. Some people have a particular dislike of visiting the doctor and may put up with all sorts of discomfort to avoid this. In such a case there may be a build up of multiple health problems, some of which may only become apparent when the elderly person loses the regular support they received from their partner. For example, someone whose eyesight has been failing may have managed adequately and even kept their poor sight a secret whilst the partner was around to help out but when they are forced to live alone problems arise.

Poor sight, bad teeth, neglected feet and deafness are health problems which are all worth tackling, as sometimes small adjustments like a stronger pair of spectacles or treatment from a chiropodist may be of immense help and enable the person you care for to live a more independent, better quality life.

If the person you care for has any of these minor health problems check out the facilities in the area where they live. The first point of information is the GP surgery and the district nursing service (sometimes called the community nursing service). Be persistent. Some GPs may be vague about what is available and unfortunately too aware of their budget restrictions. Some are uninterested in the elderly and their problems. Generally the district nursing team are likely to be very helpful and will be able to point you in the right direction. Major changes are taking place in the area of district/community nursing, particularly in the area of elderly care, and there is a big push to improve 'care in the community' to ensure that more elderly people are able to continue living at home and avoid undue hospitalisation. Like many NHS initiatives it is a money saving exercise but there are many benefits to the elderly person wishing to live independently at home. As with other services, the availability and variety of facilities offered differs from area to area (for example, the person in charge may be called a 'modern matron' or a 'team leader' depending on the area) but the district nursing team will be able to tell you what is available for your Cared-for. There are also often helpful leaflets or notices in the GP surgery that can tell you what is available.

We bought a raised toilet seat and frame for my mother-in-law and fitted grab rails in the bathroom at our own expense She found them useful but it was only a few months later when we had to call in the district nurse on a health matter that she told us that a proper occupational therapy assessment would have recommended exactly the right height seat and frame for my mother-in-law and that we might have been able to obtain these aids free of charge. We didn't know this level of service was available.

Problems with vision

For some visual problems, a sight test and a new prescription for spectacles are all that is needed. It is not generally known that optometry (sight tests) can be done in the home for those who are unable to leave the house. However, the facilities are usually better at the optometrist's practice. If you speak to the receptionist at your Cared-for's local optometry practice beforehand, they will very often make special provision for an elderly person with exceptional difficulties. For example, you might ask if you can use the staff car park if your Cared-for cannot walk far. All optometry centres will be able to provide information about free eye tests, and help with provision of spectacles for those unable to pay. If the person you care for is partially sighted many aids are available for everyday living (see Chapter 5 on First Steps – OT aids and equipment). In addition, it is worth contacting the various associations for the blind to see what they can offer (see Further information, page 34).

My elderly aunt was told during an eye examination that the optician had noticed some changes and that he would refer her to her GP as she might need treatment for diabetes. She didn't understand at all. It was only after we asked questions on her behalf that we realised that the eye examination can show up many incipient medical problems (for example, diabetes).

Hearing

Hearing tests are available at home in the same way as sight tests, but again the equipment is better at the hearing centre. The district nursing team will be able to tell you what is available but your Cared-for may need to be referred by their GP. Many private companies offer hearing tests and hearing aids and some of these are an improvement on what is available on the NHS. (Be warned: if you send to hearing aid companies for any catalogues you may remain on their mailing lists for life.)

Chiropody
Again, this is supposed to be available to those who are elderly and/or housebound and who also have an additional heath problem from visiting 'domiciliary' services. This means that they will come out to treat your Cared-for at home. Ask the district nursing team what is available in your area.

In conclusion

It may need some pressure on your part to get these services and unfortunately those who make the most fuss are the most likely to get the most complete help. Do not be put off by stories of understaffing or long waits for treatment. Your Cared-for has the right to these services. If they have to wait this is still better than getting no help at all. Again, persistence pays off. If you know your Cared-for has been placed on a waiting list check regularly to see what the position is.

For the more active elderly, treatment for minor problems, dental work, occupational therapy and physiotherapy, and even some out-patient services, may be supplied at local 'community' hospitals which are more accessible and pleasant to visit than large general hospitals. Many areas offer a transport service (staffed by volunteers) to get people who are not car drivers to doctors, out-patient appointments and therapeutic services. The GP surgery should have details of this service if you ask (see Chapter 4 on Getting about.)

If the person you care for has the means and can pay for private treatment the whole process may be quicker and simpler. Again, the GP surgery may carry lists of local practitioners of chiropody and physiotherapy and they will probably be prepared to come to the home if necessary, but it will be expensive. If you need to find practitioners yourself, local libraries, telephone books and, increasingly the internet are good sources of information.

Further information – service utilities

Independent Occupational Therapy
Occupational therapists in independent practice
For tips about qualifications to look for when using private practitioners.
www.otip.co.uk
0800 389 4873

The Outside Clinic
Offers eye tests and an eye care service in your own home
www.outsideclinic.com
0500 295 245

Wiltshire Farm Foods
Deliver frozen ready meals to your home
www.wiltshirefarmfoods.com
0800 773 773

Women's Royal Voluntary Service (WRVS)
Meals-on-wheels and social transport schemes; a good neighbour scheme for minor household repairs
www.wrvs.org.uk
01235 442900

Foundations
Information on local Home Improvement Agencies to help older people stay in their own homes
www.foundations.uk.com
01457 891909

Public Guardianship Office
Information about Power of Attorney
www.guardianship.gov.uk
0845 330 2900

Rotaract
The 'active' branch of Rotary Clubs for younger members
organises activities such as gardening and helping the elderly
www.rotaract.org.uk
Local telephone numbers

Lions Clubs International
Local volunteer helpers
www.lions105m.org.uk
0121 441 4544

The Scout Movement
Local groups may be prepared to give active help to individual
elderly
To find your local groups contact the national HQ
http://www.scouts.org.uk/
0845 300 1818

3

Financial matters

Including benefits and entitlements

My mother could cope perfectly well with all her everyday living needs but she had never managed the finances – apart from the cash sum my father passed to her for housekeeping purposes. She was sound in her mind and able to understand money matters but had never dealt with banks, cheque books or cash cards (and did not want to learn how to). She wanted me and my brother to do that part for her.

This chapter looks at ways in which you as a carer might help your relative or friend, your Cared-for, with managing their finances. A significant section covers Enduring Power of Attorney. Making arrangements to cover fees for care or nursing homes is discussed and there is also some information about various benefits and entitlements.

There are still many partnerships where only one of the partners takes charge of the everyday management of money and if your Cared-for was not the one who routinely looked after finances they may view the prospect of taking on the handling of bank statements, cheque books, standing order/direct debits and debit/credit cards with dismay. How you help to resolve this will depend upon your relationship with them of course. Some people will need just a little help with understanding how financial institutions work and others will want to hand the entire 'package' over to someone else.

Joint bank accounts

If your Cared-for had a joint account with their partner then, as discussed in chapter 2, it is easily converted on the death of one partner into the sole name of the survivor. If your Cared-for has not been used to handling a bank account and wants help, then it might be worth discussing with them at this stage the possibility of transferring the account into joint names with you, their carer. You can arrange for all actions on the account (including paying by cheque) to need both account signatures or you can arrange that the signature of either one of you is sufficient. Dual signatures might reassure someone who wants to feel in control of their money but single either/or signatures may make it simpler if your Cared-for is ever unavailable (for example, in hospital) to sign when necessary. If you do not bank with the same bank as your Cared-for, than the bank will want to see proof of your identity when you convert the account, just as if you were opening an account in your sole name.

Savings accounts and securities

Usually savings accounts and securities can also be put into joint names and again the best time to do this is when the account name has to be changed anyway. The procedures will be similar to changing to a joint bank account and any financial institution will want various proofs of identity from you as above.

Benefits payments

If your Cared-for is in receipt of benefits that are normally paid into their bank or building society account and they are unable to collect cash from that account on a temporary basis, they can write to their bank or building society, asking them to give temporary power to someone else to operate their account (see above, Joint bank accounts). If their benefit is normally paid by cheque, they can fill in the back of the cheque to allow someone else to cash it for them. If your Cared-for wants their carer to cash a benefit cheque for them on a regular basis, they should contact the office that deals with their benefits payments to let them know.

Power of Attorney

Power of Attorney (POA) is a legal process in which someone (the 'donor') hands over to someone else (the 'attorney') power to decide what is done with their finances and property. An Ordinary Power of Attorney can be used to authorise an attorney (generally a relative or friend) to carry out all tasks for the donor. Alternatively, the donor can use an Ordinary Power of Attorney to grant *limited* powers to an attorney, for example to buy and sell property, to change investments or to enter into a contract. A Limited Power of Attorney must be drafted in very clear terms to ensure that the powers really are limited to those authorised by the donor.

There is no standard form for an Ordinary Power of Attorney, and if your Cared-for wants to grant an Ordinary Power of Attorney, it is best to contact an experienced adviser, for example, a solicitor.

I was looking after my confused, 90+ year old mother. Since most of the money was in my name I did not think that I needed

Power of Attorney. However, my cousin wanted to wind up what had become a small fund established by our grandfather and this needed my mother's signature. Because she was incapable of understanding, or even signing, I applied for Power of Attorney, not knowing the difference between the various kinds. I was granted Ordinary Power of Attorney, but it proved that this did not authorise me to sign on her behalf as she was now mentally incapable of administering her own affairs. She was too confused for me to obtain Enduring Power, let alone register it, so we were in a dilemma and I was not very popular with my cousins. Immediately after this I gave Enduring Power of Attorney to trusted acquaintances for myself! So far no-one has needed to use it.

However, an Ordinary Power of Attorney is no longer valid if your Cared-for becomes mentally incapable. An Enduring Power of Attorney (EPA) on the other hand differs in that it it will remain valid should this happen to your Cared-for (provided it is registered with the Court of Protection (COP)). Anyone can make an EPA, but in order to do so a person needs to be mentally capable of making the decision to take this step and if you are using a solicitor s/he will not go ahead unless s/he is sure of this. If your Cared-for is not mentally capable of making an EPA see the section below (Court of Protection).

Your Cared-for can give their 'attorney' (the person to whom they are entrusting their finances) complete power over their financial affairs or they can put restrictions on that power. For example, they can specify that their attorney cannot sell their house without permission.

The forms to set up an EPA can be obtained from the Court of Protection or downloaded from their website. There is also a very helpful booklet available from the Court of Protection, which explains the EPA and the procedure for setting it up. The Court of

Protection makes it clear that you do not have to use a solicitor to set up the EPA. The signing of the forms by your Cared-for and yourself in front of witnesses is sufficient. Unless your Cared-for specifies otherwise on the form, once you and your Cared-for have signed the form and registered it with the relevant banks and financial institutions that administer your Cared-for's money, the EPA is in force.

You are likely to find, however, that the people you deal with in the said banks and financial institutions are unaware of this rule. They are likely to demand that the document is signed and sealed by a solicitor. You may therefore decide that it is easier to use a solicitor to make the arrangements in the first place.

My mother set up an EPA naming me as the attorney. We lodged the document with the solicitor who had helped set it up for safe-keeping, but years later when we wanted a certified copy to give to the bank he refused to send me one. We wrote and telephoned several times but he said that he was not able to release the document without my mother's agreement. As my mother was suffering from dementia by then, we wanted to lodge the EPA with the Court of Protection and even they could not understand why the solicitor wouldn't give us the document. Eventually, he only handed over the EPA when the Court of Protection threatened to intervene directly. If we had to do this again I would retain the document myself.

Whether you use a solicitor or not, it may be advisable for either you or your Cared-for to retain the signed document yourself in a safe place. Banks will not keep the original copy for their records but they will not accept a photocopy made by you. You will need to take the document into the bank and let them make a copy which they will certify as a true copy and retain for their records.

If your Cared-for loses their mental capacity and you hold an EPA, then you must register it with the Public Guardianship Office (PGO) or Office of Care and Protection (Northern Ireland). You have an absolute duty to do so, and you may not use the Enduring Power of Attorney until you have applied to register it. After you have applied to register the EPA, but before the registration actually happens (it can take a while because the PGO (Office of Care and Protection in Northern Ireland), has to wait to see if anyone objects), you will have limited authority to maintain the donor and prevent loss to their estate.

Before you apply to register the EPA, you should give notice of your intention to do so to the donor and to the donor's nearest relatives. This is because the donor and their relatives are entitled to object to the registration of the power or to you as the attorney. There are standard forms that you must use and certain classes of people whom you have to notify. For example, if you notify one child of the donor you must notify all children. The PGO or Office of Care and Protection will supply the forms you need (or you can download them from their website) together with the exact instructions about notifying and registering.

You also have to certify that you have notified the donor, even if they are unable to understand the notification. You send the notification forms to those who should be notified and there is then a period of time in which they can object to the appointment of the nominated attorney. However, the PGO is not likely to accept a frivolous objection and would want substantial reasons why you should not be appointed since you were the person your Cared-for wished to appoint as attorney when they signed the EPA. There is, of course, a fee to be paid for the registration, but this can be paid from your Cared-for's funds.

If there are no objections (or if the PGO overrules the objections), the EPA is returned to you signed and sealed. This signed EPA must now be registered with all the financial institutions where your Cared-for has accounts. You do not need to (and should not) part with the registered EPA. Take it physically to each institution and they will make a 'certified photocopy'. If your Cared-for holds postal building society or electronic accounts than contact the institution to find out the procedure. Normally you can have a certified copy made at a local high street branch of the relevant institution for forwarding on.

Banks and building societies differ in their procedures. Some will just note the EPA on their records and some will close the accounts in your Cared-for's name and open new ones entitled, for example, 'J Smith POA for Mrs M Smith'. If this is the case, new cheque or pass books will be issued for the account. Many banks will not allow a cash (debit) card on POA accounts, which may make it more difficult for you to manage the affairs of your Cared-for. It is difficult to understand the reasons for this since you can of course draw cash by signing a cheque on the account when-ever required.

When we registered the POA for my mother-in-law, the bank withdrew her debit card and would not issue one on the new account. When I enquired why, I was told that it was because, due to her mental incapacity, she might 'draw out all her money'. When I pointed out that it was her money and she was entitled to do so they didn't really have any answer. They promised to write to me with an explanation but never did so.

Once you have registered the POA it is best to keep careful records of your management of your Cared-for's money. The Court can ask to see your records at any time, although they seldom do so. You also have a duty to keep your Cared-for's money and financial affairs separate from your own. You now have the power to set up and cancel direct debits and standing orders on your Cared-for's behalf (see Chapter 2 for information about paying utilities by direct debit), to write cheques and to withdraw cash and spend it for their benefit. You also have the power to make cash gifts if this is something your Cared-for would normally do. For example, if Granny always gave a Christmas present of cash to her grandchildren you can make similar gifts on her behalf from her funds. However, you should be careful to use your Cared-for's money in a responsible manner in accordance with the instructions given by the PGO when granting the registration.

An EPA may appear to give wide-ranging powers, but you should note that they are purely financial. For example, you may be able to claim benefits on your Cared-for's behalf, but you cannot make medical decisions for them. You do not have the right to decide where they should live (although in practice, because you manage their financial affairs, you may be able to do so). You cannot make a will on their behalf, nor change a will which they had made at an earlier date. Perhaps surprisingly, you cannot nominate another attorney if you no longer feel able to carry out these duties. If you wish to relinquish your POA, the Court will nominate another attorney. (In practice they usually nominate a close relative but it may not be the one of your choosing.) The point is that it was your Cared-for who chose the attorney and you cannot change their decision.

Paying for nursing home fees

I knew that my mother would probably have to fund part of her nursing home fees but frankly I was horrified to realise how expensive these would be and, of course, we had no idea how long the funding would be needed. We consulted a specialist financial adviser. One of the surprising things was that Mum could invest a lump sum and be assured of her fees being covered for as long as she lived. She found it hard to make the decision to use such a large sum, but in the event she (and we) did achieve peace of mind for the last seven years of her life. We were happier to see her use the money to ensure her own comfort than to try to save it to pass on to us.

When and if the time comes to consider moving to a residential care home or a nursing home, your Cared-for, like many older people today, may not meet the criteria (detailed in Chapter 11) for state financial assistance for care/nursing home fees, or they may choose to enter a care home independently of any state aid. However, their available capital, perhaps savings or the proceeds from the sale of a former home, if left in a high interest deposit account, may not yield sufficient income to meet the high costs involved. Consequently, many people find their money runs out long before their need for care ceases. But there are specialist care fees advisers who can help with planning for care home fees. You and your Cared-for may find it useful to consult one of these.

Firstly, competent advisers who understand the complexities of Local and Health Authority support, DWP benefits, tax efficiency and legal arrangements can ensure you and your Cared-for are aware of your proper entitlements. Secondly, such advisory firms will provide your Cared-for with appropriate financial advice so that they can afford their chosen type of care.

The financial products that are appropriate for meeting care costs vary according to an individual's age, health, required income and the degree of risk a family is prepared to take. Proper advisors aim to identify financial products that deliver returns significantly above those provided by deposit based savings, but without taking undue risks with capital. It is worth consulting such an adviser if it is clear that your Cared-for may need nursing home care in the future.

Ideal financial products are those that can provide a regular income and incorporate flexibility to meet any future changes in care needs, for example, fee increases or the additional cost of moving from a residential care home to a nursing home. The ultimate aim might be to enable care costs to be met for the life of your Cared-for whilst, as far as possible, preserving original capital, independence and, if your Cared-for wishes, as many people do, the ability to leave an inheritance.

Good questions to ask a financial advisor/about a financial product concerned with care/nursing home fees are:

1. Does the product provide fees indefinitely or only for a limited number of years?
2. Does the product provide for increases in fees?
3. How much will my Cared-for need to invest?
4. Will this product give more security than a simple investment of the funds available?

Benefits and entitlements

> The District Nurse advised me to find out if my mother could claim the Attendance Allowance. Whist I was researching that I discovered that I could claim Carer's Allowance myself as I had left my job in order to look after Mum. This led me to search further and I found a whole range of entitlements which Mum could get and which we hadn't even known about.

Many people fail to take full advantage of state support or make decisions to claim or not to claim without fully appreciating the consequences. There are a number of different benefits to which your Cared-for might be entitled. Some are listed below with a short description of the circumstances in which they can be claimed. The whole benefits area is very complicated and sometimes you can actually end up worse off over all because you claim a certain benefit. The following list is only meant to give you a starting point to investigate what might be available. Telephone helpline and website addresses are given where possible to help you with further research. The Citizens Advice Bureau can also help. In fact, 'benefits advice' is one of the major reasons the public give for consulting the CAB. In order to apply for most benefits you will have to complete application forms, but most have been designed to be as simple and easy to understand as possible. In some cases you can complete and sign the forms on behalf of your Cared-for; in other cases not. The Department of Work and Pensions, which deals with most benefits, has a dedicated enquiry line.

Age related benefits

Pension Credit
If your Cared-for is aged 60 or over they may be entitled to Pension Credit – extra money each week. It is made up of two elements – the 'Guarantee Credit' element and the 'Savings Credit' element (which may be payable from age 65).

Freephone 0800 99 1234

www.pensions.gov.uk/pensioncredit

Over 80 pension
The Over 80 Pension is a state pension for people aged 80 or over who have little or no state pension. Unlike other state pensions, it is not based on National Insurance contributions.

Disability and caring related benefits

Carer's Allowance
A taxable benefit for informal carers aged 16 or over spending at

least 35 hours a week looking after someone who is getting or waiting to hear about Attendance Allowance, Disability Living Allowance, or Constant Attendance Allowance.

Attendance Allowance
Paid if you need help to look after yourself, and/or if you become ill or disabled on or after your 65th birthday, or are claiming on or after your 65th birthday.
Paid at different rates depending on whether you need care during the day, during the night, or both.
www.dwp.gov.uk/lifeevent/discare

Heating and energy use

Winter Fuel Payment
You'll automatically get Winter Fuel Payment if you're aged 60 or over and live in the UK. People over 80 who are entitled to Winter Fuel Payment will get an additional payment.
Winter Fuel Payments helpline: 08459 15 15 15
www.thepensionservice.gov.uk/winterfuel

Cold Weather Payments
Made during periods of very cold weather if you or your partner are:
- getting extra money on Income Support or
- getting income-based Jobseekers Allowance or
- getting extra money because you are aged 60 or over
- or are long-term sick or disabled or
- getting Pension Credit

Warm Front scheme
Offers grants for insulation and heating improvements
Freephone 0800 072 0151

The Anglian Water Trust Fund

An independent charitable trust established in 1996 which aims to contribute to the fight against poverty within the Anglian Water region.

Grants are available to help individuals and families in need meet arrears of water and sewerage charges and other household bills and costs.

Tel: 01733 421021

www.awtf.org.uk

Housing and general living benefits for those on a low income

Housing benefit

Sometimes called rent rebate or rent allowance, this is paid by local councils [Question: under what criteria?].

You do not have to get any other benefits.

Council tax benefit

Help towards your council tax, whether you rent or own your home, or live rent-free.

Paid by local councils as a rebate on your council tax bill. (You do not have to get any other benefits and it does not matter if you already get a discount on your council tax, for example because you live alone.)

For information on Council tax benefits see

www.dwp.gov.uk

or telephone your Local Authority

Social and entertainment

Free TV Licence

If your Cared-for is aged 75 or over they're entitled to a free television licence. If they're 74, you can apply for a short term

licence to cover the months until they reach 75. Your Cared-
for can also get TV licence concessions if they're living in
residential care.

Tel: 0870 241 6468

Further information – financial matters

Benefits Now
This site enables you to assess yourself for Disability Living
Allowance or Attendance Allowance before you apply. You can
find out whether you qualify and at what rate you are likely to
be paid.
www.benefitsnow.co.uk

Nursing Home Fees Agency
Specialist care fee advisers
Tel: 01865 733000
www.nhfa.co.uk

Citizens Advice Bureau
The Citizens Advice service helps people resolve their legal,
money and other problems by providing free, independent and
confidential advice.
Local telephone numbers can be found on their website or via
directory inquiries.
www.citizensadvice.org.uk

Department of Work and Pensions Benefit Enquiry Line
Confidential advice and information for people with disabilities,
and their carers and representatives, about social security benefits and how to claim them.
Phone: 0800 88 22 00 (Free)

4

Getting about

This chapter aims to deal with the problems and solutions to getting about for generally able elderly persons. The discussion covers the frail, less mobile and easily tired elderly. If your Cared-for has a specific long term disability, specialist advice is needed and there may be an association or specialist health therapist who can advise you about their needs. For this reason discussion about wheelchairs and electric scooters is not covered at length here.

Getting about is often a problem even for the fit elderly and you as a carer may be heavily involved in this aspect of your Cared-for's daily life. The problems incurred, and their solutions, fall into different categories depending upon whether your Cared-for is a car driver or uses public transport. This chapter will also consider the problem of walking and general mobility. As advised in previous chapters, do not rely solely on information and aid from 'official' sources. Many local groups and charities offer support and help in individual cases. Your local library and the internet are the best sources of information about these. It may be particularly worth contacting any charity or voluntary organisation linked to the profession to which your Cared-for may have belonged. Several of these organisations are listed in the reference section at the end of the book.

Driving

Driving licences have to be renewed at three yearly intervals for those over the age of 70 years. If your Cared-for holds an old style 'paper' driving licence they will be automatically sent a D46 and D750 reminder application forms 90 days before their 70th birthday from the DVLA. They must complete these application forms ensuring that all the relevant questions are answered. They will need to enclose original documentation confirming their identity and a passport style colour photograph.

If they are a photocard driving licence holder they will only be sent a D46 reminder application form 90 days before their 70th birthday. They must complete the D46 application form ensuring that all the relevant questions are answered but there will be no need to enclose any identification or photograph.

The likely reality is that your elderly relative or friend will be over the age of 70 and will already be in the three year renewal cycle. Sometimes the DVLA require a report or an examination by a GP or even a specialist doctor. Doctors are entitled to make a charge for a medical report or a medical examination and they are required to list their charges for these services in a public area of the General Practice premises. Most GPs are sympathetic to the needs of their elderly patients and many will not charge them even though they are entitled to do so. If your Cared-for would find difficulty in paying it is always worth approaching the GP to request that they waive the charge.

It is worth checking that your Cared-for is not paying out needlessly for certain other items. For example, they are exempt from paying the Vehicle Excise Duty (Road Tax) if they get:

- The higher rate of the mobility component of Disability Living Allowance.
- War Pensioners' Mobility Supplement.

If they are eligible for these exemptions but not able to drive themselves they may nominate another person's vehicle (for example yours) to be exempted from tax. To qualify for exemption the vehicle should be used substantially for the purposes of the disabled person.

If your Cared-for gets the higher rate of the mobility component of Disability Living Allowance or War Pensioners' Mobility Supplement, they should automatically be sent the exemption forms.

Otherwise you or they can contact the DVLA for details, or see their website.

The Blue Badge scheme (formerly the Orange Badge scheme)

The main purpose of the scheme is to allow disabled and blind people to park, or be parked, closer to their destination. When a vehicle is parked, the Blue Badge should be displayed so that the holder's name and the date of expiry are visible. The person entitled to have a badge may be a driver or a passenger. This means that you could display the badge on your car if you are driving your Cared-for about.

The Blue Badge generally means that you can:

- Park without charge or time limit at parking meters.
- Park without a time limit in streets where waiting is allowed for limited periods.
- Park on single or double yellow lines for up to three hours. In Scotland there is no time limit.
- Park in designated 'Blue badge' disabled parking spaces in public car parks.

However, a Blue Badge is not a licence to park anywhere. Some restrictions do apply and the above is for guidance only. For example, you cannot park in bus lanes, cycle lanes, when loading restrictions apply, etc. You will need to read the full instructions that you or your Cared-for receive with the Blue Badge.

It is an offence to display a Blue Badge if the disabled person has not been in the vehicle prior to its being parked, unless the driver is parking to collect the disabled person. So you should not have the badge on display whilst you are using the car solely for your own requirements.

Your Cared-for can obtain a Blue Badge if:

- They get the higher rate of mobility component of Disability Living Allowance.
- They get War Pensioners' Mobility Supplement.
- They use a vehicle supplied by a government department or have a grant towards the running costs of their own car.
- They are registered blind.
- They drive regularly and have a severe disability in both arms which means they cannot turn the steering wheel by hand.
- They have a permanent disability so bad that they cannot walk or they have great difficulty in walking.

Contact the social services department of your local council. They may ask your doctor (GP) for medical evidence about the degree of disability.

Or see the Department for Transport's website for full information (see page 66).

If your Cared-for does not hold a Blue Badge you may still feel that they (or you if you are driving them) should be able to park in a disabled bay because, for example, they have difficulty in walking the distance from the normal car parking spaces to the relevant shop or amenity. You or they should not park in a 'Blue Badge' space unless the car has a Blue Badge displayed. However, some shops and car parks have spaces which are labelled 'for disabled use' and not specifically for Blue Badge holders. Most shops and supermarkets will be sympathetic if you use these spaces to save your Cared-for a tiring walk.

Holding a driving licence does not mean that your Cared-for is fit to drive. Vision problems may have worsened over the years but not been reported to or recorded by the GP. Minor strokes may have occurred and not been recognised. Movement in the limbs may have been affected to a degree which makes it unsafe to drive. This is one of the most difficult areas for carers. On the one hand the ownership of a car and the ability to drive confer a huge element of independence on your Cared-for. You as a carer are also relieved of the problem of arranging transport for everyday activities. On the other hand, driving (even locally and over well known routes) is an activity fraught with danger if undertaken by someone who is not medically fit to drive and the danger is not just to the driver but to other road users and pedestrians.

My mother only used the car to do her local shopping and go to the hairdresser and so on. She was always driving on familiar territory and I didn't think there was a problem. But one day she had a minor bump in a car park and hit her head. She then abandoned the car and was found by the police wandering around the shopping centre. When we talked it over it became clear that she shouldn't be driving any longer. The police said that they would not prosecute provided we sent her licence back to the DVLA and that she didn't drive again. She was 81 at the time.

If you are not sure whether your Cared-for is fit to drive look out for the following signs:

- Driving at inappropriate speeds, either too fast or too slow
- Asking passengers to help check if it is clear to turn left or right

- Responding slowly to or not noticing pedestrians, cyclists and other drivers
- Ignoring, disobeying or misinterpreting street signs and traffic lights
- Failing to judge distances between cars correctly – for example, driving too close to the vehicle in front
- Having one or more near accidents or near misses
- Drifting across lane markings or bumping into curbs
- Forgetting to turn on headlights when they are needed
- Having difficulty with glare from oncoming headlights and streetlights, especially at dawn and dusk
- Finding it difficult to turn to look over their shoulder to reverse.

It may be very difficult to persuade your Cared-for that they should stop driving but if they become unfit to drive or decide to give up it is not all bad news. For one thing, sale of the vehicle may bring in a useful capital sum. There is no longer a need to worry about servicing and repairs and insurance policies, and roadside rescue agreements can be cancelled. If you are a driver yourself, your Cared-for may opt to keep the car and have the insurance changed to your name so that you can have use of the vehicle to take them out when required.

Alternatives to driving

When my mother-in-law could no longer use the car she agreed to let my son have it on permanent loan on condition that he drove her out on errands or to the local shops etc. We had to ensure that he understood that a condition of the loan was that he gave his Grandmother's needs priority but overall we all benefited from the arrangement. There were fewer calls on our

> time, he gained the use of a car which he would not otherwise
> have been able to afford and in fact he became, over time, very
> fond of his little excursions with her.

At this stage you might give consideration as to what needs your
Cared-for has which actually require some form of transport.
Often you can cut the need to a minimum with a few lifestyle changes. For example, most doctors surgeries will send
completed prescription forms to the pharmacist of your choice
and many pharmacists will deliver the made up prescription free
to your relative's house. Several large supermarkets offer an
on-line ordering service and home delivery of groceries and
household articles. If your relative cannot use a computer you can
make the order on their behalf. This is very convenient as heavy
shopping is delivered right to the door at a time of your/their
choice. Mail order shopping is an expanding area either through
catalogues which come to the door or via web pages – virtually
anything can now be ordered without leaving home.

Of course, your Cared-for will not want to be confined to the
house unnecessarily and getting about without a car is now much
easier for elderly people thanks to the many local council schemes
in operation. Contact your local council to see what they offer. In
particular, ask about the following:

Local bus travel

Local travel for elderly people is now free in many areas (usually
outside of the rush hour) but you will have to find out how this operates in your locality. Some local authorities offer 'tokens' which can
be used on buses and in parking meters and are often accepted by
local taxi firms. Others issue a renewable 'pass' which needs to be
produced for each journey. If your Cared-for is still mobile and lives
in an urban area then local buses may be of immense use. Routes

nearly always operate from outlying areas into town centres to allow for shopping. Frequently the buses will stop 'on request' to allow passengers to alight near home, and local drivers may come to know their regular passengers well and be prepared to help with parcels and shopping. Many public vehicles also now have wheelchair and 'lift' access for those who find climbing steps difficult. In rural areas the bus services may be less frequent but many small outlying communities now benefit from local enterprise in the form of 'post buses' or special transport laid on with the elderly non-driver in mind. In many areas, both in town and country, special buses are arranged and paid for by large 'superstores' to allow shoppers to come to them. Most large hospitals also have some sort of 'shuttle' bus service from outlying areas. Where local post offices have recently been closed down local councils have sometimes arranged for special buses to be run to enable customers to reach the nearest post office from small villages or outlying areas. Find out about these and similar arrangements by contacting your local authority or your local library.

Dial-a-ride and similar arrangements

This type of arrangement (there are a variety of descriptive titles depending on where you live) is sometimes operated by local councils either through a contracted service or sometimes by volunteers. Dial-a-Ride services provide door-to-door transport for anyone who finds it difficult or impossible to use ordinary public transport. You don't have to be registered disabled or confined to a wheelchair to use Dial-a-Ride type services – for example, you might have difficulty climbing steps on buses, or be unable to walk to the bus stop. Dial-a-Ride type service vehicles can also carry passengers in wheelchairs. Fares are about the same as you would pay on ordinary buses. Your Cared-for will need to book journeys well in advance to be sure of a seat. They will be collected from their door at the arranged time, and the driver will help them into the vehicle. Usually vehicles are equipped with a lift or ramp which can be used by anyone who has difficulty in climbing steps.

A number of voluntary organisations both local and national provide transport for individuals in various areas. In most cases, these services rely on volunteer drivers who may be reimbursed a mileage rate when using their own car. Passengers will generally be asked to contribute towards the cost of this transport, although rates will vary between organisations. The type of service provided is often confined to lifts to doctors' surgeries or to local hospitals for outpatient clinics. Details of these volunteer services can usually be obtained via your local council or from your local library. Volunteers will sometimes also provide an escort service into the outpatients department if, for example, your Cared-for is unable to cope alone.

Train travel

Most train companies have arrangements for disabled passengers and this may include those who just need a little extra help to get on and off trains or find the right connections. The train companies can usually arrange for staff to meet your Cared-for at their departure station, accompany them to the train and see them safely on board. Similar arrangements can be made at the destination station and other stations if there is a need to change trains. For example, ramps can be provided for wheelchair users or wheelchairs between platforms for those who are mobile but cannot walk far. You will need to contact the individual train companies to find out details. Sometimes you can obtain details at the local station ticket office but often you may find you have to ring a special 'enquiries' number. Most train companies are better able to help if you contact them as far in advance of the journey as possible. Look on individual websites or contact train companies by phone or enquire at local stations' ticket offices.

Taxis

If your local council provides 'tokens' instead of bus passes, these are often accepted in payment by taxi services. Many taxi services are extending their fleet of vehicles now to include cars with ramps or let down steps to make it easier for elderly and disabled persons to use them. The local council usually carries details of taxi firms with facilities for the disabled on their web site or you can get this information in leaflet form at the local library. Businesses such as hairdressers and restaurants will usually agree to telephone for a taxi for their customers to return home after an appointment and may know which taxi services are most helpful to the elderly or disabled.

Local informal arrangements

Don't feel that you have to find 'official' transport for your Cared-for. Often friends and neighbours are happy to help out with a lift to the shops, to a lunch club or a day centre. If your Cared-for is a regular churchgoer a word with the vicar, priest or minister will usually ensure that a lift to church can be arranged with another parishioner as nearly all churches operate some sort of lift/shared transport scheme. Similarly if your Cared-for regularly attends at a local club or association and is no longer able to drive to meetings an approach to the organisation will often result in the offer of a lift to meetings.

Visiting shops and other amenities

Your Cared-for, although not actually disabled, may tire easily or simply be very frail. They may enjoy outings and visits but need extra help in getting about, in finding articles on sale or simply need to sit down frequently. Most large supermarkets and garden centres now supply free loans of wheelchairs for customers who need them. If the wheelchairs are not obviously on view it is always worth asking if they are available. Some shops may not be able to keep them near the entrance. (There is even a growing trade in stealing wheelchairs from store entrances so some traders may prefer to keep them under supervision when not in use.) Tourist attractions such as stately homes, gardens and cathedrals also have wheelchairs for hire or free loan. If you are planning a visit it may be worth telephoning in advance to reserve a wheelchair where this is allowed. Smaller shops and businesses now have, by law, to make suitable concessions to help those who are disabled or less mobile. This may mean that they simply display a notice saying that they will give assistance if asked. Take advantage of the law and do so! Most shops will supply a chair for frail customers to sit down, for example. Larger supermarkets often provide an accompanied shopping service where a member of staff will walk around the store with your Cared-for and reach things from high/low shelves and carry the shopping basket. The biggest obstacle you may encounter when trying to arrange such help is resistance from your Cared-for. They may hate to be seen as 'disabled' or in need of help.

My mother suffered from heart failure and got out of breath very easily. She could walk, but not far and only very slowly. It was frustrating for her and for us because she loved shopping and visiting local attractions but kept denying any need to use a wheelchair. One day she visited my sister for a few days and my sister informed her that she had hired a wheelchair for her to use 'just so that you can visit the cathedral'. Mum loved old churches and accepted this suggestion as a 'one off'. After this she was converted and happily chose to use free wheelchairs when visiting big stores and the local garden centre.

Personal comfort

Elderly people may need to use the toilet more often than others. Not all public toilets are open when needed and most do not have facilities (raised toilet seats, for example) that your Cared-for may need. A very useful scheme is operated by RADAR (Royal association for Disability and Rehabilitation) whereby you can write to them with your Cared-for's details and they will supply, for a nominal cost, a key which opens the locks of around 4000 disabled toilets in car parks and public places throughout the UK. You have to put the request in writing in order to explain why your Cared-for needs the key but they do not have to be registered disabled to apply – having stiffness from arthritis, for example, is sufficient. This is an extremely useful amenity. Many elderly people avoid leaving home even if they would enjoy an outing because they are afraid they will need the toilet at inappropriate times.

Walking aids

There are now many types of walking aid available although they may not all be available free of charge.

Walking sticks

The varnished wooden stick is attractive and traditional. However, many different designs of walking stick are now available. For example, you can get a stick with a 'crutch type' armrest for someone who needs this. You can also get sticks with a tripod foot for greater stability. A tight grip is required to gain support from a walking stick, so these are only suitable for people who are still reasonably mobile and strong. If you are unsure, your local physiotherapy department will give advice on the best type of walking stick for each individual; you may have to get a referral to the physiotherapist through the GP or district nurse.

Zimmers

There are two main varieties of Zimmer – a 'box-style' frame with rigid legs, and a frame with two front wheels to allow easier movement. The classic box-style Zimmer is very stable and easily gripped, but it requires two hands and is cumbersome to transport. These products have been so dominant as aids for the elderly, that the 'Zimmer', just like the 'Hoover', has become a household name.

There are, however, many different types of walking aid available now which make the traditional 'Zimmer' seem almost archaic.

Trolleys

You can obtain shopping trolleys which have an added seat and this is ideal for someone who gets tired easily but is otherwise able to get about and do their own shopping. Your Cared-for can place purchases inside the carrier, and rest on the padded top for a short time if walking becomes too tiring.

Rollators

Rollators have wheels which allow you to turn and pivot in a way that trolleys cannot. Rollators are a lightweight yet sturdy walker alternative. There are many different types. It may be best to look through a catalogue or check the various websites before deciding on the one for your Cared-for. An even better solution is to visit a showroom and try out various models. However, if this is not possible almost all vendors operate a postal order and delivery service, often with next day delivery. In general they are very reasonably priced.

These 'rollators' and trolleys can make a big difference to your Cared-for's sense of security, comfort and convenience both inside and outside the house. They are light weight and the dimensions are such that they can usually be easily used around the house. Some have a seat if the user needs to sit and rest for a moment. Users can also sit and move about with their feet on some models (for example, while working in the kitchen) and they all fold up for convenient storage in the car boot or a cupboard. Some have a tray incorporated for carrying meals and drinks around the house, others have a basket (rather like a bicycle basket) so that packages, books, plants etc can be moved safely.

My mother was very obstinate about using a stick even though it was clear that she was very 'wobbly' on her feet. She would drag herself around the house clutching walls and doorframes. When she went out she would hang on to one of us. But when she spotted a three-wheel 'trolley' in a magazine small-ad she decided it was the very thing. And it was. She could use it inside and outside of the house and it seemed to give her back a sense of independence.

For those who find walking even a short distance difficult or uncomfortable there are a range of electrical scooters and power-chairs available. Some of them are lightweight and will fit into the boot of a car. They are not a cheap option but the cost may well be worth it to you and your Cared-for.

Temporary support equipment

If your relative requires temporary support equipment for getting around, the NHS is responsible for providing 'personal mobility aids'. For temporary walking aids, your relative will usually need a recommendation from a physiotherapist who will advise on the right equipment. Referrals to physiotherapists can come through any of the following:

- local hospital
- community health service (district nurse)

- local health centres
- doctor (GP).

So, for example, if your relative, or friend, has been admitted to hospital with a fracture then when they are discharged the hospital will ensure that the physiotherapy department measures for and provides the correct equipment to help your Cared-for get around. If they have a fall at home and perhaps just need some extra support to help them walk until they recover fully, then the best thing might be to ask about referral to a physiotherapist through the GP or district nurse.

The NHS provides mobility equipment on loan. It is not allowed to charge for equipment, but in some cases your Cared-for may be asked to pay a returnable deposit to ensure return of the item. In some cases this system has been introduced because loaned crutches, for example, and other small items, are frequently never returned to the hospital from which they have been lent.

Aids and equipment needed for long term use may be obtained, after assessment by an occupational therapist, from your local social services department. She or he will also be able to advise you about voluntary organisations and private companies that may also be able to help.

For very temporary use (for example, during a holiday visit from a relative) the Red Cross provides a hire service.

Several companies manufacture mobility equipment. An occupational therapist from your local social services department may be able to give you advice about such companies and also voluntary organisations who may give grants towards equipment. But if you do not want to contact social services most of these commercial companies advertise freely in magazines, newspapers and on the internet. Do not think that because they are commercial organisations these companies are selling inferior equipment. Most are reputable firms who rely on recommendation to retain custom and many have their own advisors to help you choose the right aid for your Cared-for. Remember to specify to the seller if your Cared-for has a disablity (they do not need to be registered disabled) and then they may be exempt from paying any VAT (Value Added Tax) on equipment.

Getting upstairs

For some elderly people getting upstairs is the only difficulty. They can walk around, carefully and slowly perhaps, and they are able to drive or use public transport as required. But for one reason or another they cannot climb stairs. Sometimes the problem is not the stair climb itself but the length of time it takes to negotiate the stairs. For example, if the only lavatory is upstairs this may make considerable difficulties for an elderly person with bladder problems or indeed for anyone on diuretics, which tend to create 'urgency incontinence'. There are grants available to allow disabled or infirm people to make adjustments and improvments to their home which will allow them to continue living there. First port of call once again is your local library or local council website or enquiry service. For example, your Cared-for might be eligible for a grant to convert a downstairs room into a toilet or bathroom.

If your Care-for is totally unable to climb the stairs and a move to ground floor accomodation is out of the question than the classic answer is the stair-lift. As with mobility aids there are a number of firms which supply these and your Cared-for may be able to get a grant towards the cost. It is not widely known that many suppliers will renovate and supply second hand stair-lifts which cut the cost considerably for the buyer. You or your Cared-for should be sure to ask about this when investigating a stair-lift as not all companies will tell you this up front.

Before investing in the expense of a stair-lift it is worth you checking very carefully that your Cared-for will be able to use it.

Some mobility problems will mean that this is not an option. This also applies to elderly people with early dementia who may not be able to learn to use the stair-lift properly.

There are many very simple steps you can take to help your Cared-for to be more generally mobile or to make the most of the mobility they have. Things like ensuring good lighting around the home, preventing clutter on stairs and in passageways, and installing extra handrails may make a big difference to general ease and comfort. More details about these steps are to be found in Chapter 5, First Steps.

The following references are examples of suppliers of information and equipment to aid the elderly in getting about. To find out what transport schemes are available in your area the best recommendation is to contact your local authority direct or ask for information in your local library.

Further information – getting about

Department for Transport
General information about transport facilities for the elderly
www.dft.gov.uk

Information about the Blue Badge scheme
www.direct.gov.uk/DisabledPeople

Royal Association for Disability and Rehabilitation (RADAR)
Tel: 020 7250 3222
www.radar.org.uk

Stair-lifts

Stannah
Tel: 0800 715 171
www.stannah.com

Brooks stairlifts
Tel: 0800 834730
www.stairlifts.co.uk

Walking Aids

Uniscan Walkers
Tel: 0800 0640762
www.uniscan-walkers.co.uk

Able Mail Order
Tel:0800 358 0445
www.independentliving.co.uk/able/mailorder.html

5

First steps

Occupational therapy assessment, aids and equipment

My parents-in-law had seemed completely self-sufficient. I had noticed that he seemed to be getting rather autocratic with her but just put this down to 'old age crankiness'. Then he was taken ill with pneumonia and we all realised suddenly that she was quite incapable of looking after him properly. He had been compensating for her memory lapses and loss of ability by giving her direct instruction all through the day. ('Get up now, Freda,' 'Get ready to go shopping now,' 'Give me your washing to put in the machine.') We had honestly no idea until then that she was suffering from the beginnings of dementia.

Sometimes we see at an early stage that elderly relatives or friends need a little help. In some cases they will voluntarily ask for help, but very often they will not, seeing it as a weakness (a sign of growing old!) or as an imposition on younger family or friends to ask of their time. It can be a small thing that makes us realise – noticing difficulty with carrying shopping, for example, or realising that they are reluctant to leave the house or to pay visits. Very often an elderly couple will become used to compensating for weakness in each other. The wife will start driving the car when her husband has been the main driver up until then, because he says one day that he is too tired. In reality perhaps he realises that his vision is not as good as it was. Or perhaps the husband starts to do the supermarket shop because his wife begins to forget essential items. Unless they are very close and visiting every day these small adjustments may go unnoticed by friends and family until a crisis happens.

Frequently the sudden illness, admission to hospital or death of one partner brings a shocked realisation to the relatives, friends or neighbours and 'crisis management' has to be resorted to. Family and friends may not realise that there is help available or they may find that the elderly person continually refuses to accept 'charity'. There is often a horror of 'free' help or anything that smacks of 'social security'. Frail people about to be discharged from hospital may refuse all help, insisting that their family can 'do all that is needed'.

We knew Mum and Dad were getting more frail but they seemed able to manage on a day to day basis and one or other of us was always around at the weekend. But one weekday I finished work early and dropped in. The house was freezing cold. The fire which ran the central heating via a back boiler had gone out. It was tricky to light and Dad had always been in charge of the job. But on this day he had put his back out and was unable to get out of his chair. I found Mum in tears trying desperately to light the fire under his increasingly irate instruction. She had arthritic hands and couldn't manage. This incident made the whole family think more carefully about how they could help.

It is very worthwhile at this stage to get together and agree co-operation as a family, or a group of friends. Lack of co-operation may turn out to be the biggest underlying problem. Resentment and hostility quickly build up in the absence of communication.

Guilt plays a part. A daughter living at some distance away may really resent the 'hands on' care given by a daughter-in-law even whilst knowing and understanding that she is unable to give it herself. A son may not feel at all able to give this kind of care and react by belittling the care given by his sisters.

Group meetings early on, where concrete plans can be made and (if possible) where recriminations are withheld will help avoid such situations developing. If someone lives too far away to help with daily care perhaps they can agree to come and stay at intervals and give 'holiday cover' to the chief carer. Someone who is not good at practical personal care may instead be able to manage the financial affairs. It helps to make use of personal strengths here. Someone who enjoys cooking may agree to keep the Cared-for's freezer stocked with ready meals whilst someone who is only free once a week but is a car driver might organise the shopping. A family member who works within the health service may act as the co-ordinator for healthcare.

If you appear to be the only person available to help with care you should not try to take on everything alone. There may well be neighbours or friends of your Cared-for who will help in the same way that family might do. Otherwise you will have to turn to professional help. Indeed, some elderly people prefer the notion that any help they are receiving is 'paid' help and not done as a favour.

There are a vast number of practical things that can be done to help your Cared-for live independently for longer. Occasionally elderly people becoming aware of their increasing difficulties will arrange help for themselves. Otherwise it may fall to the Carer to do this. The following information is meant as a guide to what is available.

Occupational therapists

The services of an occupational therapist are usually available free of charge and you can gain access to their help through your local council, your GP or community nursing service, or through social services. Occupational therapists (OTs) are trained to assess the ability to manage everyday tasks and to give advice on selecting aids and appliances or making adaptations to the home environment which might help. You can ask for an OT assessment for your Cared-for. If she or he has spent some time in hospital (following a stroke or a fall, for example) then they are unlikely to be discharged from hospital until an OT assessment has been carried out. Most community hospitals have units where they can check on the ability of patients due for discharge to carry out simple tasks (such as making a cup of tea), but if your Cared-for has been in hospital for some time, and particularly if they live alone, the OT team will probably take them home for a visit of a couple of hours during which time they will carry out the assessment. If you can arrange it, then it is worth being present at the assessment so that you can bring up any concerns you have.

A thorough assessment will include a check of the home surroundings and in his or her report the OT will note if such items as ramps or grab-handles need to be provided and point out potential hazards such as loose rugs or trailing cables as well as guiding your Cared-for through some everyday tasks and recommending aids and equipment which might be helpful. OTs are especially helpful if major items like stair-lifts or wheelchairs need purchasing. It is important that you ask to see a copy of the OT assessment report. It has happened that the report has been sent directly to the GP and is never seen by the family. It will be dutifully filed on your Cared-for's notes and you may never gain the full information you need.

If you cannot get OT advice quickly by any of the routes listed above, then you might consider using a private OT service, but for this of course you will have to pay.

Your Cared-for may be upset, or even hostile to the OT assessment, thinking that it is aimed at proving that they cannot manage and will have to 'go into a home'. The very opposite is true and you should try to reassure them. There is now a big move towards 'care in the community' and the OT team will be trying to ensure that every help is given to ensure that your Cared-for can manage at home for as long as possible.

Basic help to make everyday life easier

Even without an OT assessment or purchasing any aids, you as the Carer can make sure that your Cared-for's home is safer and more convenient for them.

Lighting is very important. Replace light bulbs promptly and use the highest wattage which the light shade and fitting allow. Consider free standing or wall mounted spotlights near to chairs used for sitting to read, knit etc. Make sure that stair lights can be switched on and off both at the top and the bottom of the stairs and that halls and passageways are very well lit. A light coloured paint or paper on the walls helps to make the most of the light. Kitchens may need extra 'spot' lighting around food preparation areas and bathrooms near mirrors.

Stairs and hallways need to be kept clear of clutter as much as possible and again pale floor coverings help to make obstacles more visible. A second hand rail can be fitted to most staircases if required (on the wall side). Small rugs should either be taken up or backed with non-slip matting or backing. Loose edges to carpets should be fixed firmly down.

Grab rails can be fitted quite easily by someone reasonably competent in DIY. These can be bought using specialist mail order catalogues or ordered on-line and are very useful in the bathroom and around front and back entrances, especially if there are any steps to be negotiated.

If you look around the house with your Cared-for you may both agree on some simple and helpful changes which can be made without too much trouble. Think, for example, about moving frequently used objects to a lower cupboard (but not too low if there is difficulty bending), choosing to use a table lamp with a more convenient switch, using a gas or electric fire rather than an open fire, sanding down sticky drawers or doors so that they open without using excessive force. These are small changes, they cost little or nothing and they are usually easy enough to make without difficulty or causing hostility.

Special aids and equipment for kitchens and general cleaning

There are many aids available to allow easier use of the kitchen. For everyday cleaning up, long handled mops and brushes and dustpans are invaluable and save bending (see Figure 1). You can often buy these in large DIY stores or ironmongers shops. Disposable cleaning cloths and disinfectant wipes (although

Figure 1 Long-handled dust pan and brush

Figure 2 Screw-top opener   **Figure 3** Jar opener

expensive) save spills from rinsing cloths out. These are available in most supermarkets. A smaller washing up bowl will weigh less when full of water than a large one. Special tap-turners can be obtained which make it easier for arthritic hands to use the taps.

Many available items make food preparation safer and easier (see Figures 2 and 3). You can get non-slip mats for placing under bowls and chopping boards, kettle tippers to obviate the need to lift a kettle full of boiling water, and grip-cloths which give a non-slip grip on the tops of jars and bottles. There are special devices available to enable your Cared-for to open 'ring pull' cans more easily and angled kitchen tools to make food preparation easy. You can purchase revolving shelves to make it easier to access cupboards.

For those with limited vision, it is possible to buy packs of adhesive strips or discs of bright coloured or fluorescent material. These can be stuck around control knobs, or switches to make them easier to see. Counter tops can be edged with bright strips too.

If a major item of equipment such as a cooker or microwave oven is to be purchased it is worth giving first consideration to how easy it is to use. For example, a self-igniting gas cooker (although expensive) ensures that the gas is not left unlit by mistake. Microwave ovens are available with large figures or digits on the controls to help those with visual difficulty. Some washing machines operate by pushing a button rather than turning a dial, which may make life easier for someone with limited hand movement. Fridges especially need to be examined to see how convenient it is to reach inside and whether the shelves are contoured to make cleaning easy. There are extra light vacuum cleaner models available or a simple carpet sweeper could be used for everyday.

There are some small items of furniture which can make a big difference to life. A step stool with a hand-rail can help to reach high cupboards, a perching stool will make life easier when preparing vegetables or other food, a trolley walker which incorporates a tray eases carrying things from room to room. You can also get 'free hand' trays with a carrying handle, and beanbag eating trays which enable lap top eating from a stable surface.

For eating and drinking a whole range of specially adapted cutlery (see Figure 4), plates and mugs are available which make it easier to eat or drink one handed or with a weak grip.

Figure 4 Two forks

Bedroom aids and equipment

The height of the bed is very important. Bed height can be raised with special raisers but if the bed needs to be lower you may need to buy a new one.

When my Mum first equipped her cottage after Dad died it seemed clear that a high bed would make it easier for her to get in and out and at first this was ideal. What we didn't realise was that after her stroke she had real difficulty lifting her bad leg into bed and this slipped the notice of the OT assessors too. Once she told us about this we bought a lower bed as a replacement and installed a rail to help her get out of bed from the lower height.

You can get all sorts of back rests to make sitting up in bed more comfortable. One of the cheapest is the V shaped pillow, which can also be used in a chair. It is very good for those who need to sleep with head and shoulders raised and pillow cases can be bought with it for easy laundering. This pillow can be bought in many high street stores. You can also buy rigid back rests for use on a bed, which will fold flat for storage. Wedge shapes can be purchased to raise the foot of the bed to relieve swollen ankles. Over-bed tables (see Figure 5) can be obtained with castors which make them easy to push aside and make eating or reading in bed easier. There are also specific disability bed aids which help with sitting up or getting out of bed. The OT will advise on the best if needed.

There are various aids available to help with dressing such as button hooks, stocking and sock helpers and zip pullers. The extent to which people find these aids helpful appears to vary widely. However, one small and simple aid for someone who finds

Figure 5 Bed tray

bending difficult is the elastic shoe lace. In appearance it looks like a normal lace but it enables shoes to be put on and removed without bending or difficult lace tying. You can buy these through mail order catalogues or online (see Further Information, page 84).

Special aids and equipment in the bathroom and toilet

The bathroom is one area where there seem to be more aids and items of equipment available than in almost any other area. Using these items may take time but they do allow those with disabilities or stiffness of the limbs to be independent and this is an area where most people wish for privacy. It is worth experimenting to find what items work best.

Bathrooms and toilets in modern houses are usually fitted with locks which can (in an emergency) be opened from the outside. These locks are also available from DIY stores and hardware shops to be fitted to existing doors and are well worth it for the Carer's peace of mind.

My husband suffered a heart attack whilst using the toilet. Luckily I heard him fall and was able to open the bathroom lock from outside using a screwdriver. An ambulance was called by my daughter, who was visiting at the time, and he was taken to hospital and survived the attack. I was just so glad we had locks which could be opened from outside.

As mentioned in the kitchen section, tap turners are available and these can be fitted to bathroom taps for those who have trouble turning taps on and off.

There are many aids to help with washing oneself. Long handled sponges and cloth grippers help with washing the back or the feet. Back washing cloths with easy to hold handles are also available. For foot washing you can obtain special toe sponges which enable you to wash between the toes without bending. A flannel glove is often easier to use than a face flannel for hands which cannot grip easily. Liquid soap dispensers may be easier to use than a slippery bar of soap, although you may have to test several makes to find one that is stable and does not need too much pressure to release the soap.

Walk-in showers are the ideal solution to bodily cleanliness and there are many items which can make showering easier. Grab rails will help stability when standing and for those who find this difficult shower stools are available which will withstand constant wetting. It is also possible to have a fixed shower seat installed which will fold away when not in use, although this is a more expensive option. There are some designs of shower which dispense with the shower stall 'lip' but again these will have to be specially installed and may be expensive.

Many elderly people do not use a shower, either because none is installed in their accommodation or because they prefer and are used to using a bath. At the very least you should ensure that your Cared-for has a non-slip safety mat to use in the bath. Bath rails which clip to the side of the bath will also assist to give a safe and secure handhold. There are simple portable bath steps available which just make the task of getting in and out of the bath easier. For those who have more difficulty there are bath boards, bath seats, and raising and lowering devices which may help. This is an area where the OT can give most helpful advice. Bath cushions will help those who find the hard surface of the bath uncomfortable.

Nearly everyone would prefer to remain independent when using the toilet. The most obvious aid in this respect is the raised toilet seat. This can be fitted to the toilet in minutes and add between 2 and 6 inches to the height of the seat, which may make life considerably easier for a frail elderly person. You can also either fit grab rails next to the toilet or purchase a toilet frame which will have an adjustable height and arm rests. This makes sitting on and getting off the toilet a lot easier. Bottom wipers are obtainable for those who have difficulty turning or reaching behind them. These are designed to hold the toilet paper and are adapted for hygienic removal of the paper after use. They will also hold moist toilet tissues and so are useful for general hygiene purposes.

It is very easy to assume that a daily bath or shower is essential and become very concerned if your Cared-for cannot manage this. It should be remembered, however, that the daily bath or shower is a comparatively recent convention. It is possible to have a thorough all-over wash which will be as effective as a bath or shower and if this replacement for the daily bath or shower keeps your Cared-for happy and independent, it is worthwhile.

It got to the stage where Mum just couldn't manage to climb into the bath. She didn't like showers so one of us would go once a week to help her bath. On the other days she would lay a big bath towel over the bath mat and standing at the basin give herself a

---

thorough wash using a long handled sponge. She could manage this without help and was delighted to continue to be independent in this manner.

Dealing with incontinence

Issues with incontinence in dementia are covered in Chapter 9, Dealing with dementia. However, some elderly people suffer from incontinence for physical reasons. They are aware of the problem and are able to deal with it. Doctors sometimes talk about 'urge incontinence' and 'stress incontinence'. Urge incontinence is when the sufferer has to go to the toilet in a hurry. It may happen due to weak muscular control or it may be due to diuretic medicine (sometimes known as 'water pills'). Stress incontinence happens when urine leaks out whilst the sufferer is laughing or sneezing or perhaps getting up suddenly from sitting down or exercising. It may not matter very much which type of incontinence your Cared-for has. You and they are likely to be more concerned about dealing with it on an everyday basis. All the previous suggestions about raised toilet seats and grab rails/arm rests apply here along with any other adjustments which make it quicker and easier to use the toilet. Raising you Cared-for's usual chair to make it quicker and easier to get up will help, and so will making sure that they wear easily adjustable clothes such as loose skirts, elasticated-waist skirts and trousers, roomy pants and stockings, or pop socks rather than tights. Press stud or Velcro fastenings, which can be undone quickly and easily, will be useful.

There is a big range of incontinence wear available ranging from small 'stick on' pads for small leaks to fitted pads and waterproof pants. If these are needed you do not have to go to a specialist shop to get them. They are available in most supermarkets as well as from pharmacists or by mail order. If you or your

Cared-for are not sure what to use or buy then consult your district nurse. In most areas there is a specialist 'Continence Advisor' who is usually a trained nurse and who can visit your Cared-for and help to decide on the best way to cope with this problem. You can ask your Cared-for's GP or the district nurse to arrange a referral to the Continence Advisor.

General living

There are many aids available to assist in independent daily living. Key turners which fit over the key end will help stiff hands to turn keys. Likewise, knob and handle turners fit over door handles to make them easier to turn. Long handled milk bottle holders mean that no bending is necessary to pick up the milk. Internal letter catchers can be fitted inside the front door. Cordless phones and phones with large buttons or large size numbering will make using the phone easier. Special loop handles can be fitted to electric plugs to make them easier to grip or you can obtain cheaper add-on or stick-on devices. An electrician can raise the most used sockets so that no bending is required to reach them. Special smoke alarms and door and telephone bells can be purchased which flash instead of sounding for the hard of hearing. It goes without saying that remote controls for TV, video and music centres will make life easier and all of these can be bought with larger than normal buttons to make them easier to see and use.

Raising your Cared-for's favourite chair may make a big difference to them when it comes to standing up and sitting down, and it is possible to buy inexpensive chair raisers for this purpose. If affordable, a rising/reclining chair will make life even easier. These can be manually or electrically operated and will help someone who has stiffness or who is unsteady to stand up in a controlled manner. They are very expensive to buy new as they are often made to order. However, you can try to obtain one second-hand.

When it comes to safety, a simple door chain costs very little, is easy to fit and will give reassurance when answering the front door. (However if carers or visitors normally let themselves in with a key, then your Cared-for must not leave the chain in place all the time. You could put a sign up by the door to remind them to use the door chain before answering the door themselves.) A TV security camera can be bought for quite a small expense and fitted via the TV to allow your Cared-for to view who is at the door before they even open it. Outside lights with sensors which come on if someone approaches the house are simple to fit and not very expensive.

Personal alarms are very useful if your Cared-for is liable to fall or to need help when they cannot reach a telephone. These usually have a central unit and help can be obtained by pressing a button on this unit. They also incorporate a satellite unit which your Cared-for can wear as a bracelet or a pendant. A permanently staffed call centre will answer if the call button is pressed and either advise your Cared-for or call out the best helper – the Carer or the emergency services, for example. Unfortunately these alarms are not a good solution if the user is so safety conscious that they might inadvertently switch off or unplug the unit or if they suffer from dementia and cannot understand or learn what to do in an emergency. Also, there are many elderly people who object to wearing the alarm, though some modern ones are relatively small and can more easily be hidden under their clothes. You will need to discuss with your Cared-for whether this is the most appropriate emergency aid for them.

Medicines are usually dispensed in bottles with child resistant caps, but you can ask at the pharmacy for an ordinary screw top bottle. 'Organisers' for pills, which help the elderly person to remember to take them on time, are available – some very simple – some very sophisticated. For those who have trouble swallowing pills, it may be possible to have a liquid alternative. It is important to ask the doctor about this if it is needed because the doctor may not even think of this eventuality.

In the garden

If your Cared-for is a keen gardener there are a multitude of aids available to help them enjoy their garden Strangely enough, many of the best aids will be found in specialist gardening catalogues rather than in 'disabled' equipment catalogues. Many simple adaptations to the garden will help, such as raised beds, extended patio/hardstanding areas and pot raisers.

For those who suffer from a specific disability, any of the appropriate organisations which offer support in that area will be able to offer more specific information about aids and equipment. For example, many aids are specifically designed for those who are blind, partially sighted or deaf and these may not be available through general disability centres or shops and catalogues.

Finding and obtaining aids and equipment

This chapter has been written to give general advice about the help, in the form of aids and equipment, which is available. It is unfortunately not possible to give specific advice in a general work of this nature. Items of equipment can be obtained from many suppliers. Some things are obtainable free via the health service or social services and some are available for hire at low cost through organisations like the Red Cross or through charities. You may like to do initial research via the internet and then follow this up by seeing the equipment and trying it out. There are Disabled Living Centres and shops in many towns where items can be examined and tried out and where assistance and advice is on hand to help you decide what to purchase. A great many things can be purchased through local pharmacies. Some sources of supply are listed in this chapter's Further information section (see below). If money is short it is also worth investigating what is available locally either free or on long-term loan. Many local councils offer lending schemes and churches and other local charity groups may offer renovated second-hand equipment.

Further information – first steps

Disabled Living Foundation
Provides information and advice on equipment. There is an Equipment Demonstration Centre with large displays of equipment which visitors can try out and where advice can be obtained.
Helpline – 0845 130 9177 (charged at Local Call Rate)
Equipment Demonstration Centre – (020) 7289 6111 ext.247
www.dlf.org.uk

Assist UK Disabled Living Centres
A network of centres around the UK which provides information and advice on products and where you can see and try our products.
Tel: 0870 770 2866
www.dlcc.org.uk

British Red Cross
Ability Catalogue – products for independence
Tel: 0870 739 7391
www.redcross.org.uk

Incontinence Products
Tel:0800 180 4325
www.dryforlife.co.uk

Lloyds pharmacy
Local pharmacy branches stock catalogues of aids and equipment and can order items for you and have them delivered to your nearest pharmacy. The website has a 'nearest pharmacy' search facility.
www.lloydspharmacy.co.uk

BenefitsNow On-line shop
For elastic shoe laces and other aids for living
www.benefitsnowshop.co.uk

Gimble – hands free reading device
www.gimbleuk.com

Independent Occupational Therapy
Occupational Therapists in Independent Practice
Tel: 0800 389 4873
www.otip.co.uk

RNIB
Royal National Institute for the Blind
Tel: 0845 702 3153
www.onlineshop.rnib.org.uk

RNID
Royal National Institute for Deaf People
Tel: 0870 789 8855
www.rnidshop.com

6

Social needs

Mum and I had always been very close and often shopped or had outings together. After Dad died, however, she seemed to rely on me entirely for all her entertainment and company, refusing to go out to the club she used to frequent and to accompany neighbours shopping as she had done before. I found it really difficult because I had my husband and children to look after as well, and there simply wasn't enough time in the day for all her 'demands'.

Elderly couples often come to rely on each other for company and entertainment and take up hobbies that they can enjoy together. Gradually old friends may die or move away and they may become isolated without even realising it. If one of the couple dies it may be a real shock to the survivor to discover that they have so few outside contacts. Many elderly parents turn to their children and younger family to fill the gap in social life. This can put heavy demands on whoever is the main carer.

Another difficulty which sometimes arises is when previously physically fit elderly people become less fit and cannot socialise as they have been used to do. Sometimes the physically fit member of the partnership dies first and the surviving elderly person finds difficulty in carrying on the social life which they enjoyed before simply because there is no one to fetch things, drive them out or help them to do what they previously did together. Again the main carer may find they are under pressure to supply the missing help.

This chapter examines the social needs of the elderly who are living alone and suggests ways in which these needs can be met by and shared amongst their carers.

Accept any help offered

After a bereavement it is natural for family to take extra care of the surviving relative, to give more time to them and to arrange activities which will please and distract - to try and 'fill the gap'. It is quite common for help offered by non-family or those seen as 'outsiders' to be refused in the early days. The family may feel that the bereaved person can only cope with close relatives or friends and probably have the intention of asking for help after a short time has passed. However, help which is refused may not be offered again as those offering may feel rejected. It is also human nature for offers of help to come flooding in at times of crisis and to tail off as things seem to be getting back to normal. It is very important for the immediate family, and especially for the main carer, to encourage their Cared-for to keep in touch with old friends and acquaintances and to take up again any regular activities.

If neighbours and friends offer help, therefore, do not turn it down. One very good solution is to ask them to do something specific, give a lift to the shops, have a shared meal or drop in for coffee once a week, for example. Or you could ask a neighbour to accompany your Cared-for on their first visit back to a regular club or church. Do not be put off if your Cared-for at first says that they would rather do these things with you. It is important for them to re-establish a wider social life and it is important for you to have alternative helpers to call on at need.

If help is not offered remember to ask for it. Neighbours may hold back because they are afraid of interfering or members of social clubs or groups may feel embarrassed and not wish to intrude. But many people welcome being approached and asked to help and are glad to feel that they can do something which is practical and useful.

Start with the immediate environment

When considering social needs and any changes which need to be made, start with the immediate environment. However often your Cared-for is taken out or visited they have first to get used to the new condition of living alone and furthermore in an environment where reminders of their previous life and companionship are constant. You may spot small changes around the home which if made would really help your Cared-for in their daily life (see Chapter 5 on First Steps). However, don't suggest changes too soon after a bereavement as it may upset your relative or friend, who may like the comfort of still seeing their partner's chair in its regular position or their dressing gown hanging behind the bedroom door. Things which will provide distraction and prevent too much morbid thinking will be useful. If a daily paper was not delivered before then your Cared-for might like to arrange this now as it makes a useful routine to the beginning of the day. The daily postal delivery will probably be looked forward to much more than before and there are many ways to enhance this experience. Relatives who live too far away to visit can be encouraged to send letters and postcards regularly. A magazine subscription can give a regular lift in spirits and mail order cata-logues which may be seen as a nuisance to those of us leading busy lives outside may be looked forward to with enjoyment by someone with time on their hands. Your Cared-for might like to join a book club and receive regular books in the mail or perhaps to take up a pen friend with regular letters to look forward to. You and your Cared-for might like to consider daily past-times and hobbies and how these can be enhanced. If your Cared-for is a reader and used to make regular trips to the library then this can be continued. If they are a non-driver and the library is at some distance investigate whether there is a mobile library van which calls locally. This is an excellent service and usually operates even in quite remote areas. The mobile library carries a good selection of books and will take orders for borrowing just like the main library. They will also stock large print books. Your local library and your local county council will have details of mobile library services. Alternatively, perhaps you could arrange for a neighbour to take your Cared-for to the library regularly. This would provide an outing and a chance for social contact as well as the pleasure of selecting books to read. An avid reader who is happy to use a computer would probably enjoy ordering books via the internet. Do not dismiss the idea of introducing your Cared-for to computers and the internet. Personal computers these days are very user friendly and you certainly do not have to be particularly technically minded to use them. As suggested below, a teenage member of the family may really enjoy showing grandma or grandpa how to use a PC.

After my mother died we used to order books for Dad via the internet. He began to get very interested in the way we did this and eventually invested some money in a PC and internet connection which my teenage son set up for him. It gave him a whole new lease of life and he spent hours on the web and even used some chat-rooms! He also emailed the grandchildren frequently and got a lot of pleasure from their replies. On birthdays he even used to send 'E cards'.

Many elderly people enjoy both television and radio pro-grammes. It may be that they have carried on for years using a particular model of radio or television because they have become used to it and have never considered updating their systems. Newer systems may offer a larger screen, easier controls, clearer sound and an improved enjoyment of the media. If your Cared-for enjoys music encourage them to upgrade their music system and to use CDs instead of tapes both for ease of use and for the sound quality. CDs can also be borrowed from the library. Video machines and DVD players offer a range of entertainment.

For all entertainment media consider how best the equipment can be placed to make it easy to use for your Cared-for, taking into account their lifestyle and abilities. For example, if your Cared-for has difficulty bending down it may make sense to place the DVD or video machine on a table or shelf beside the TV rather than on the shelf which is often provided below the TV stand. If your Cared-for particularly likes to listen to the radio in the early morning then it may be more important to have the radio in the bedroom than the main sitting room, or perhaps to have an additional radio. Your Cared-for may enjoy watching TV in bed and an easy to use remote control may be important here.

For those who have poor sight, consider talking books. There is now a vast range and they can be obtained in most high street stores and can be borrowed from the library in both tape form and as CD. They are also a very useful present idea. Many news-papers and magazines can be purchased in a spoken form (see Further information, page 99) and arrangements can be made for these to be delivered regularly by post.

My mother was partially sighted and after she died I was left with a large collection of talking books which I felt were far too good to just throw away. By chance I heard of a lady who attend-ed my church and who had developed an eye condition which prevented her reading. I offered her the collection and she was delighted. But there was a knock-on effect. Someone else in the church hearing about this began to run a lending library of talking books and quite a number of people benefited. Some had books to pass on and some wanted to borrow. I always felt that my mother would have approved of her 'legacy'.

Plan a pattern to the day

When newly bereaved, a pattern to the day can be a great help for someone living alone. A daily pattern will also help someone in the early stages of dementia to remain orientated. Mention has already been made of the daily paper and the postal delivery. If a cleaner or a professional carer comes in, then the times which are arranged are also part of the day's pattern. You could usefully help your Cared-for to plan their radio programmes or TV viewing as part of this pattern and to incorporate exercise such as a short walk or even a stroll around the garden daily. Meals also break up the day. The main meal might be best taken in the middle of the day because this will be better for the digestion, especially if your Cared-for goes to bed early. A mid-day meal is also the best arrangement if your Cared-for uses meals-on-wheels or has a carer come in to cook the meal. The preparation of meals and snacks can be a very pleasurable activity and a good opportunity to incorporate short visits. A neighbour might drop in regularly mid-morning for coffee or you might arrange your daily visit to coincide with tea-time. Further tips on keeping up a good standard of nutrition and making simple meals can be found in Chapter 8 on Problems with nutrition. A weekly pattern which incorporates regular shopping trips, visits to social clubs or to church or visits from family members will also help your Cared-for.

Encourage any hobbies

> Most of their social life for my parents centred around their local
> Wine Circle which was a real social club with weekly meetings,
> visits and dinner parties. When my father died my mother con-
> tinued as a member of the Wine Circle and kept up with all her
> friends there. When she moved nearer to me a couple of years
> later she did try to join the local Wine Circle but said that she
> didn't find it very welcoming. I was really sorry because so much
> of her social life had dropped away.

Activities and hobbies

There are many ways for your Cared-for to keep up with old activities and hobbies even if their circumstances have changed. These
days almost every activity can be indulged in via post, telephone or
the internet. Some examples of how hobbies can be adapted follow.

If your relative or friend likes **crafts**, kits can be obtained by
post, as can sewing and knitting patterns and wool and materials.
Magnifying apparatus will help even those whose sight is
impaired to sew, knit or do other craft-work. Model making kits
can be obtained by mail and there are enthusiasts' clubs and
websites which your Cared-for can join.

> My mum found the wintertime with the short days and dark
> nights the greatest trial after Dad died. In the autumn she used to
> order small dolls and knitting wool and materials to dress them.
> She would work on the dolls' wardrobes all winter and in the
> spring give them away as presents to friends' children, her grand-
> children or as raffle prizes and gifts at Sales of Work and so on.
> She also made many as Christmas presents.

If your relative or friend is a keen **gardener**, nearly all garden centres cater for those with mobility problems with ramps, wheel-chairs and raised displays. Seeds and plants can be obtained by post. You can organise the garden to incorporate raised beds for those who have difficulty bending down or kneeling. Raised kneelers can be bought at garden centres and by mail-order. Long handled garden tools can also be bought. If your Cared-for has poor sight, plan the garden to include highly scented plants, clear paths made from white paving stones or gravel and well defined borders. If your Cared-for has poor hearing, external telephone bells and door bells can be fixed for those who spend considerable time in the garden. If your Cared-for has an allotment which is too big for him or her to work, then many local councils will divide plots up into smaller sub-plots among two or three persons.

Gardening was Dad's reason to live really. He had a large plot and grew all sorts of vegetables for himself and the family. When he began to suffer from angina he hated the thought that he might have to give up the garden. He bought several plastic stools and arranged them at strategic points all around the plot. Whenever he needed to he could sit down for a few moments and he could also sit down to weed parts of the vegetable beds or to sow seeds etc. This simple solution allowed him to continue gardening right up until he died.

If your Cared-for likes to follow **sport**, this is where TV and radio really come into their own. Virtually every sport is featured these days on TV and radio and if this is a favourite hobby there are magazines and papers catering for most sports and most of these can be obtained by a postal subscription or through the local newsagent. There are literally dozens of websites which are concerned with sport. Tickets for games can be bought by telephone, by post and on-line. Local sports clubs sometimes have special concessions for pensioners. A neighbour who has a similar interest might be delighted to watch a match with your Cared-for.

My mother-in-law was a racing enthusiast and enjoyed a regular bet on the horses, which my father-in-law always used to place for her when he walked down to the betting shop. After he died we helped her to continue this interest by setting up a telephone betting account (you can also bet on-line) for her and arranging satellite TV so that she could watch a dedicated racing channel whenever it took her fancy.

If your Cared-for enjoys **cooking**, they may still feel it isn't worth spending time cooking for one. You could suggest shared meals with a neighbour or friend. Allow your Cared-for to invite the family round for a meal rather than feeling that you must always invite them. Use bulk recipes to help your Cared-for stock their or your freezer. Suggest making cakes for sales and fetes. Find out about the local WI market shop or stall. Buy some of the many cookery books which specialise in cooking for one or pick up 'suggested meal' recipe cards from supermarkets when you shop. If your Cared-for is fit and mobile they might like to attend (or teach at) specialist evening classes in such things as cake icing or speciality cookery.

If your Cared-for enjoys **painting** or drawing or design, help them to set up a room or part of a room as a 'studio' with good lighting and all the required equipment. Artists' materials can all be obtained by mail order. You could help your Cared-for to set up their own website to sell their paintings or find out how to hold displays in local town centres and galleries. Paint, charcoals, paper and canvas all make good presents. Your Cared-for could join a local art club. Small local publications such as parish, school and college magazines, would welcome help from an accomplished artist or designer to arrange layout, incorporate pictures and so on.

If your Cared-for enjoys **card games** or **chess**, there are nearly always local clubs which welcome new members for chess, bridge, whist and so on. These clubs often have an informal system of giving lifts to enable less able members to come to meetings. If your Cared-for is house-bound they could host meetings. Chess and bridge can and often are played by post and via the internet, and many newspapers have chess and bridge 'puzzles' for solution. Many games have national and international enthusiasts' clubs which often issue a magazine or newsletter.

My elderly aunt enjoyed card games of any description. Neighbours and friends sometimes popped round to spend the evening playing cards but her social life really took off when she suggested a regular 'card games' session at the local day centre she attended. The people who ran the centre were very helpful and enthusiastic and eventually a separate afternoon card session was arranged. There were two 'spin off' clubs formed for different games and these started to meet in each others' houses.

Sharing the load

In many situations one family member, friend or neighbour is the principal carer. It is easy for this principal carer to fall into the way of thinking that they have to cope with all the social needs of the person for whom they are caring. This can sometimes place what seems like an intolerable burden on them. However, even family members who live at a distance or who have heavy working schedules or young children to care for can help to lighten this burden and gain a sense of being useful to their relative. Relatives or friends who live at a distance can still keep in touch and provide regular entertainment by telephone calls, letters and small gifts sent by post. Letters are particularly welcomed by elderly people living alone. Family members or friends who work full time may nevertheless be able to organise mail order and web-based shopping or may volunteer to pay for help and companionship for their relative. (It is possible to arrange for 'paid companionship'. See Chapter 10 on Professional carers.)

Family members and other friends with small children can have quite a vital part to play. There is often an affinity between young and old and if your elderly relative is reasonably fit and active they may enjoy being asked to baby-sit occasionally. Otherwise, short visits are best if children are very young and it is useful to centre the visit around something – showing Granny the video of the nursery school play or taking a present of a special cake to share, for example. Your elderly relative or friend may really enjoy photos, recordings, and pictures and cards drawn by children, and most children enjoy creating things for the elderly. Someone with young children is also in an ideal position to suggest that schools and nursery schools invite the elderly to see school plays, concerts and shows and to receive harvest gifts and so on.

Teenage children tend to be rather self-centred and may not want to bother with their elderly relatives but they can be encouraged to do shopping and small DIY jobs and many of them will be happy to purchase musical or computer equipment on your Cared-for's behalf or to give advice on the best equipment to buy, to set it up to ensure the best quality sound/picture etc.

After Dad died we wanted to ensure that Mum still felt loved and knew that we would all keep in touch. However, we agreed that in her case it would be a bad idea to arrange that one of us always called or visited on a particular day as if these arrangements fell through we knew she would be bitterly disappointed. Instead we all made sure to either phone or visit at least once a week. As there were four of us she had plenty of phone calls and visits but didn't start worrying about (for example), 'It's Tuesday and Sarah hasn't phoned yet' .

It sometimes seems that the elderly for whom we care fall into one of two groups. Those who love socialising and going out and who perhaps seem to make too many demands on the carer's time to fulfil this social need, and those who refuse to go out more than they have to and who pour cold water on any plan for outings and social events.

If your Cared-for is someone who enjoys socialising and is fit and able, then they are very likely to arrange their own social life. The problem that often occurs is that they are unable to get out and about because of an inability to drive or some disabling physical condition. Then the carer may feel that they have to be frequently on call to provide transport or help with getting about. Chapter 4 on just this subject suggests many solutions to this problem. You should also make use of any lifts offered and of transport provided by local authorities. For example, many day centres arrange transport to enable the elderly to attend their events. To find out what is available contact the individual day centre, ask at your local library or council office or use the internet to get information.

'Day Centre' is a generic term for places and organisations which provide services ranging from simple social 'clubs' with games, singsongs, bingo etc., to hot meals, chiropody, physiotherapy and day-long respite care. Some of these centres and clubs are run at community hospitals, some from care home premises and some at local church and community halls. Some are run by the Care Homes themselves as a 'half way house' for possible future residents, some are run by local authorities and some by local charities, churches and caring agencies. Each has a different character and it is worth your Cared-for trying several to find out which they most enjoy.

My friend wanted to organise visits to a day centre for her mother and asked for information at the local doctor's surgery. Unfortunately they didn't understand quite what she was asking. When she took her mother to the day centre they were both horrified as it seemed to cater mainly for old people with dementia. My friend's mother refused to go there again and unfortunately was put off ever trying another.

As well as providing entertainment and other services such centres also enable your relative to make new friends and may help to form the basis of an extended social life. However, neither you nor your relative should feel that they have to rely for a social life on clubs which cater exclusively for the elderly. Many charities welcome input from older people and most local branches of national 'interest' groups do not operate any age restriction.

If the elderly relative or friend for whom you provide care falls into the 'anti-social' category you may find yourself desperately seeking ways of providing entertainment and fulfilling their social needs. Sometimes there is a physical reason behind an apparent lack of interest in outings or visitors. For example, someone suffering from urge incontinence (needing to get to a toilet in a hurry) may not be able to contemplate going out to a place where toilets are not close at hand. Then again someone in the early stages of dementia might be actually afraid of leaving their familiar surroundings. If you are unable to establish a physical reason you may be able to take a step by step approach. For example, you could suggest and encourage a short walk, followed by a trip to the local shops followed by a longer shopping expedition. Or you could arrange for a neighbour to drop by whilst you are there and then come again and stay for a few more minutes on a subsequent date leading on perhaps to longer visits. However, it is important to remember that whatever our opinion may be about what would 'do them good' or 'cheer them up', our relatives and friends are independent people and their likes and dislikes are part of what they are. It is not the responsibility of the carer to ensure that they are entertained or forced into activity which they may not like or appreciate. If your Cared-for refuses to go out or to accept offers of entertainment it is ultimately their choice and their responsibility. It doesn't mean that you have to fill the gap by spending more time with them than you can comfortably manage.

Further information – social needs

Contact for the Elderly
Sunday afternoon tea for lonely people (restricted areas)
Tel: 0800 716543

Cruse Bereavement Care
Help, counselling and support for the bereaved
www.crusebereavementcare.org.uk
Helpline: 0870 167 1677

Boogaloo
Craft kits and hobby materials
www.Boogaloo.co.uk
Tel: 0870 787 7082

Royal National Institute for the Blind
Talking books and other products for the blind and partially sighted

www.rnib.co.uk
Tel: 0845 762 6843

Royal National Institute for the Deaf
On-line shop with aids for everyday living for the deaf
www.rnid.org.uk
Telephone: 0870 789 8855
Textphone: 01733 238020

Windsor Products
Books on 'Computing made easy' and freebies for older folk
www.windsorproducts.com
Tel: 0870 050 7791

Gardening for Disabled Trust
The Trust gives grants to people all over the United Kingdom
in order that they may continue to garden, despite advancing
illness, age or disability
Contact:
The Secretary
Gardening for Disabled Trust
Hayes Farmhouse, Hayes Lane
Peasmarsh, Rye, East Sussex TN31 6XR

7

Recognising medical conditions

Including dealing with accidents and admission to hospital

I visited Mum every day. One day calling round after work I found her sitting in front of the TV as usual but she was confused and unable to talk properly. I thought at first that she had had a fall and hit her head and I called the doctor. He explained to me that in fact Mum had had a tiny stroke. I had always thought that if you had a stroke you lost consciousness at the time and as a result of the stroke lost the use of one side of your body. The doctor explained that a small stroke might just result in a feeling like 'pins and needles' in your arm and leg, for example.

As the carer and chief person in the life of your elderly relative or friend, it is likely that you will be the one who comes into contact with them most often. There are some medical conditions which may affect the elderly in particular. They may not happen suddenly, their onset may be insidious, but the sooner they are recognised and treated the better. If your relative is not seeing a doctor regularly the symptoms may be missed. This section is not supposed to replace qualified medical help and advice but only to enable you as the carer to feel more able to make the decision to call for the doctor when required.

Also included in this section is a brief description of some of the minor medical problems to which the elderly are prone with some tips on how to relieve them.

This chapter also looks at coping with accidents and emergency admission to hospital.

I will start by looking at how to recognise:

Dementia

Conventional medical textbooks are not always helpful when describing dementia. They generally mention that it begins with forgetfulness and describe its cause but for the layman carer this is not enough. We have to recognise that elderly people are often forgetful, awkward, slow and obstinate. This does not mean that they are suffering from dementia. It is also difficult to admit to oneself that a loved one is becoming demented even if all the signs are obvious to others.

There are two recognised types of dementia in the elderly, although both can be present at once. Alzheimer's disease is the one most people have heard of and it accounts for approximately sixty per cent of cases. Vascular dementia accounts for about fifteen to twenty per cent of cases. Dementia can also result from a number of other, much more rare diseases and conditions and a dementia-like condition can result from certain nutritional deficiencies (see below). If your Cared-for has been diagnosed with one of the other primary causes of dementia such as Huntington's disease then it is likely you are already well aware of what this means. This section is aimed only at helping the carer to recognise the development of previously undiagnosed dementia.

Some medical conditions can have symptoms similar to those of dementia which is why a medical diagnosis is essential if you suspect dementia in your relative.

Dementia is progressive and gets worse over time. Symptoms are mild in the early stages and the carer can do a lot to help. Although some medical textbooks identify specific stages, particularly in Alzheimer's disease, these stages are not always present or recognisable to the untrained eye. Basically the deterioration in Alzheimer's disease is gradual and insidious whereas in the case of vascular (sometimes called multi-infarct) dementia the decline is step-like. Vascular dementia may be more easily recognised by the carer because you can observe immediate deterioration at each 'step' or minor stroke. Alzheimer's disease may go unrecognised for a long time if you are in constant daily contact with the person suffering.

As noted in Chapter 1, many sufferers from dementia are supported by their partners in such a way that the dementia is disguised or at least not recognised by even close relatives until some crisis (a death, accident or serious illness) leaves the sufferer temporarily unsupported. Here are some pointers which might make you suspect dementia in your elderly relative or friend.

Memory loss

Memory loss is more than just the 'forgetfulness' of old age. Look out for blank denials of events. 'No, my daughter didn't come yesterday,' 'I had no breakfast this morning,' even when you know that these events have happened. Your Cared-for is not being difficult. They really believe that these things have not occurred because their memory of them is lost. In the early stages they can sometimes recall events after a few gentle reminders. 'Yes, your daughter came and brought those flowers remember.' The pattern varies and many sufferers recall long ago events more easily than recent ones or can be prompted to remember by looking at photos, for example.

Sometimes people are aware of their memory loss and try to cover it up by 'filling in' the blanks. This can be very upsetting for the carer unless they realise what is happening. 'My purse is gone – the nurse has stolen it' probably means simply that the purse was put down and forgotten about. But never ignore a claim like this.

Difficulty in recognising time and dates

This is often a fairly early sign. Your relative or friend may prepare a meal for expected visitors on the wrong day, for example. They may insist that it is Saturday when it is Wednesday. Even if you point out the date (in a newspaper, for example) it may make no difference. Another sign is doing things at an inappropriate time. Your relative may telephone you in the middle of the night and not accept that it is night-time when you point this out. They may get up and dress at 10pm and go to bed thinking it is bed-time at midday. Very often people can still read the time if you point at the clock, it is just that it doesn't seem to mean anything to them. At first your relative may only mix dates and times occasionally.

Neglecting personal care

This is a very upsetting sign for most carers. Even formerly very fastidious people may neglect hygiene matters when suffering from dementia. At first your Cared-for may make excuses – 'It isn't good to put too much soap on your skin,' 'I only wear this jumper for housework – it doesn't need washing,' 'I'm too tired to wash my hair today.' Later they may not even respond when you point out dirty clothes or a lack of washing and bathing. Many people with dementia will passively allow themselves to be washed and dressed, although they will not initiate the actions. Others, especially in the early stages rigorously resist any attempts others may make to assist with personal care.

Refusal to recognise the needs of others

This may alert you at an early stage. The wife who, when her husband is ill continually complains because he doesn't take her out, the husband who demands that his wife cook a hot meal when she is unable to see to do so – these are examples of what appears to be selfishness. The carer should be alert if this is not the norm for their elderly relative.

Fears and delusions

It is not unusual for people with dementia to suffer delusions. They can also be highly suspicious and believe that others are trying to harm them or to persecute them. They may become excessively frightened. An elderly lady who has always been sensibly security conscious in the past may suddenly start to pile furniture in front of the door in case someone breaks in or may refuse to let the carer into the house 'because they are trying to kill me.' Your relative may tell you that someone they know dropped in for tea the day before when you know for a fact this is not true.

Rambling speech or inability to follow conversation

Someone suffering from dementia may not be able to explain something in a way that makes sense to you even though they are able to talk and are really trying to explain.

'It was terrible…..it just rang and ran……I didn't believe it.' (Someone came to the door and rang the bell several times.) It may take several attempts for you to understand and they may just give up the effort if you press too hard. On the other hand they may be able to carry on a simple conversation but if you make a suggestion, 'Shall we go into the garden' they may answer at random or refuse your suggestion because they just cannot make sense of it.

Inability to initiate actions

Some people with dementia find it hard to begin an action. For example, you may place a cup of tea by their side but unless you say 'Drink your tea now' they may just ignore it. Someone who is living alone and who has this problem may never take themselves to bed of their own volition or alternatively may not get up and dress without someone to prompt them.

Wandering

Many of us are familiar with the idea of the old person who 'wanders the streets' and this is a great worry for carers. As a rule those with dementia appear to be either wanderers or not. There doesn't seem to be any reasoning behind the wandering although on occasion your Cared-for may explain that they were going to the shops or 'looking for so-and-so'.

For some time we put my mother's symptoms down to other things – she was depressed following Dad's death, she needed company, old people often become frightened and confused. After all, she always offered us a cup of tea when we visited and smiled and nodded in the right places. But it was a façade. Her innate social skills were masking the fact that she could not make sense of our conversation and that although she could follow the ritual for making a cup of tea she couldn't initiate other actions alone.

Stroke

Many of us associate a stroke with a vision of someone turning purple in the face and collapsing unconscious, 'having an apoplexy' as the old books would describe it. In fact a stroke may be so mild that it goes almost unnoticed. There are two kinds. Put simply, one is caused by a 'bleed' in the brain and this type of stroke may come on gradually. Your Cared-for may complain of an intense headache which is not relieved by normal pain killers, they may start to move very slowly, to slur their words and to be unable to understand what you say to them. They may vomit.

The second type of stroke is caused by a blood clot which prevents blood reaching a part of the brain. This is likely to be more sudden in onset. Your relative may stop moving or speaking suddenly, they may fall down, their face may distort downwards on one side and they may lose the use of the arm and leg on one side. They may lose consciousness.

With any of these signs it is likely that you as the carer would call the doctor immediately. A less easily recognised stroke might be so mild that your Cared-for simply admits to feeling tired or dizzy, they may say that their arm or leg feels heavy or suffer from tingling or 'pins and needles' in the limb.

My dad complained of a headache for several days although he refused to go to the doctor. Then one day he found that the words in the newspaper made no sense to him. He slept for several hours and woke feeling slightly better. The headache gradually passed off and he was able to read again. But he had to re-teach himself some things previously taken for granted like how to tune the video recorder. In our ignorance we were just glad that he was feeling better. In fact when he saw the doctor for something else months later the doctor said he had probably had a stroke caused by a 'bleed' and that he was lucky to have recovered as he had.

Subtle signs to be alert for are:
- Difficulty speaking
- Complaints of heavy or tingling limbs on one side of the body
- Inability to use an arm or leg in the usual way. (For example, when presented with a meal your relative may just use one hand and a fork when normally they would handle a knife and fork in the traditional manner)
- Drooping of one side of the face.
- Sudden inability to make sense of printed words or of the spoken word.
- Headache which is not relieved by normal pain-killers.
- Loss of balance.

People who suffer a mild stroke may recover completely in a few hours or days or they may retain a minor impairment. Where multiple strokes happen any impairment may get worse and remain worse with each stroke (see Vascular dementia, page 142). However there is no set pattern to strokes and someone may make a very good recovery from a second stroke after making only a slow recovery from the first one.

If you suspect even a mild stroke it is essential to call the doctor. Prompt treatment is known to improve the chances of recovery.

Diabetes

If your elderly relative is a diagnosed diabetic they and you will know the treatment (tablets or injections) which they have to take and they and you will know the signs which indicate a need to call the doctor. However, in some older people diabetes comes on gradually and it is useful to recognise the signs.

In diabetes the body is unable to store all the sugar derived from the carbohydrates eaten in a normal diet. The excess sugar remains in the blood and passes into the urine carrying water with it.

Signs to watch for are:

- Excessive thirst: this can be a misleading sign. Some elderly people living alone forget to make themselves meals and may neglect to drink enough. Your visit may trigger a realisation that they are thirsty and they may appear to drink excessively simply because they have become dehydrated due to self-neglect. This is still an important feature which needs addressing by you but it is not a sign of diabetes in itself. A diabetic, however, might for example, drink two large tumblers of water or squash and still not appear satisfied, perhaps wanting another couple of glasses 15 minutes later.

- With the excessive thirst goes frequent passing of large quantities of urine. Many elderly people need to use the toilet more often simply because their bladder is weaker with age. In addition, if your relative is taking a diuretic they will often pass water frequently – usually several times within a couple of hours of taking the dose. These frequent visits to the toilet are not signs of diabetes.

- Tiredness and weakness: again, it is important to remember that an elderly person may be more tired or feel less well than when they were younger and this is normal.

- Weight loss: However, type 2 or 'mature onset' diabetes usually occurs in people who are overweight and weight loss is unusual in this type of diabetes.

- Infections in the skin such as boils or abscesses or thrush and sore feet and legs may indicate diabetes.

- Blurred vision can sometimes occur.

As indicated above none of these signs is an indicator of diabetes in itself but two or three of these signs together should suggest that medical diagnosis is required. Treatment for elderly diabetics will usually consist of attention to diet together with tablets.

Heart attacks

A heart attack occurs when the blood supply to the heart is interrupted. A major heart attack is usually unmistakable, causing severe chest pain perhaps radiating to the arm and jaw, a feeling of pressure pallor or blueness of the skin and collapse.

However, a minor heart attack when the blood supply to only a small part of the heart is cut off may produce much milder signs. Some elderly people may suffer from angina pectoris when pain in the chest comes on following undue exertion and is relieved by rest. Angina is also sometimes triggered by a large meal and may be put down to indigestion or it can be triggered by going out on a very cold day. The pain of angina varies according to the person but it will almost certainly cause your Cared-for to pause, to be unable to speak whilst in pain and to turn pale during the attack, perhaps breaking out in a cold sweat. Angina is treatable and if you suspect it in your Cared-for you should ask for a doctor's appointment without delay.

In a mild heart attack the pain is often similar to an attack of angina and there may be slight nausea with shortness of breath, pallor and a cold sweat. The symptoms may pass within minutes or hours leaving your Cared-for tired and shocked.

Because the signs of angina and a mild heart attack may pass quickly they may be easy to ignore or pass off as the signs of 'old age'. If you witness an attack and question your Cared-for you may find on enquiring that they have had several episodes which they have ignored or not mentioned to you.

Whilst living alone my father suffered what we later discovered was a heart attack one night and spent the night lying on the sofa waiting for morning before venturing to call the doctor. He later explained that the symptoms came and went at intervals but because they kept passing off and because it was night he 'didn't want to bother the doctor'.

Heart failure

Congestive heart failure occurs when the heart is unable to perform its usual functions adequately. This section will discuss gradual heart failure because sudden and acute heart failure has symptoms which would immediately cause a call for medical assistance.

In gradual heart failure there is a reduced supply of blood to the tissues and to the lungs. Because the onset is gradual, at first the body is able to compensate. When compensation is no longer adequate fluid begins to accumulate in the lower part of the body and in the lungs. The ankles and lower legs may swell and at first this may only happen after a long day 'on the feet' or in the afternoons. Later on the swelling does not go away even after a night of bed rest. Your Cared-for may get tired more easily and be unable to walk as far as before. They may also get breathless on exertion. They may need to sleep sitting up to breathe more easily. In the late stages the abdomen may swell, and perhaps the hands, and you may notice a blue tinge to the lips, ears and fingernails. In advanced stages your Cared-for may be confused and lethargic and may not be able to respond quickly enough to signals to empty the bladder or bowels.

Signs to be alert for are:
* Swollen ankles and lower legs – on more than just the odd occasion
* Lethargy
* Breathlessness
* Needing to sleep sitting up to breathe easily.

Heart failure is treatable in its early stages and your Cared-for should see a doctor if they have any of the above symptoms.

My mother's heart failure came on gradually and because the pills she was prescribed caused her to vomit she stopped taking them and consistently refused to see a doctor. My father was quite ill himself and unable to reason with her. Nor could we persuade her, although we were desperately worried. It was only when the district nurse called on a routine visit that the doctor was summoned. He explained that the dosage of the drug had to be carefully worked out by 'trial and error' and that a 'too high' dose was causing the vomiting. He gave Mum a reduced dose of her medication and she recovered and lived for several more years. However, after that we made sure that someone always went with her on visits to the doctor to listen carefully to instructions about any medication.

Concussion

Elderly people are more prone to fall over, even inside the house. A fall which involves a bang on the head may lead to concussion. Someone living alone who has a fall leading to concussion is very likely to be unaware that they are concussed. You may find that your elderly relative, or friend, is confused and suffering from a loss of memory of events just before and just after the incident which caused the concussion.

If you discover your elderly relative lying unconscious you would naturally call the doctor immediately. However, there is also the possibility that you will be their first visitor after a fall from which they have recovered and of which they have no memory.

Signs to look for are:
- General confusion
- Slurred and confused speech
- Stumbling movement and imbalance
- Loss of memory
- Visible injury to the head
- Injury to other parts of the body indicative of a fall
- Vomiting and pallor of the skin.

If you suspect concussion put your Cared-for to bed in a darkened room and call the doctor. If you suspect any serious head injury it is better to call an ambulance straight away.

Nutritional problems

Nutritional problems may be an issue, particularly if your elderly relative or friend lives alone.

Those living alone may find it too much bother to cook or prepare meals for themselves. They may only eat what they consider gives the least trouble to prepare – say a cup of tea and biscuits at frequent intervals rather than a full meal. Or they may, through lack of stimulus, always eat the same things rather than keeping to a good mixed diet. They may have a loss of the senses of taste and smell which mean that they no longer enjoy eating well. The next chapter is devoted to problems with nutrition (page 126).

CHAPTER 7

Other common medical problems

Dad was living alone and seemed to be coping quite well, although it was clear that he wasn't particularly active during the day. For several days he complained of back-ache and, thinking it was just a result of sitting around too much, we tried to encourage him to get up and walk around more and gave him some standard painkillers. Then one day when my sister was helping him to change his clothes she discovered a nasty sore on his lower back. In fact it was a pressure sore and we had to call in the district nurse to have it dressed and treated. We were told it was caused by him sitting in one position and in the same chair for much of the day.

Pressure sores

These used to be called bed-sores but they do not occur only when someone is bed-ridden. They are very painful areas of broken skin which form over bony parts of the body when the skin is pressed against bedding or furniture (a chair cushion, for example). They are more likely to happen in elderly people who are incontinent and who perhaps sit for some time in wet clothing as a result. They are also more likely to occur in people who do not move around much and spend time sitting or lying in one position. You should suspect a pressure sore if your Cared-for complains of pain in any one area especially. Pressure sores need regular dressing from the district nurse. Prevention involves encouraging your Cared-for to move around more, to change position frequently when sitting or lying down (you could encourage using different chairs to sit in at different times) to change their clothes when wet and to keep their skin clean.

Swollen feet and legs

Swollen feet and legs are not always a sign of anything serious. This swelling can occur as a result of sitting still too long in the elderly where circulation is poor. Encourage your Cared-for to keep mobile even if only around the house and suggest that when they sit they put their feet up. Relaxing/reclining chairs are very useful to encourage this.

Painful feet

Older people, particularly if they have trouble bending, may neglect their feet. This may result in long horny toenails, sores on the feet from shoes which rub and an accumulation of hard skin. It is a good idea for any carer to help wash the feet at least once a week so as to spot trouble arising. Chiropody is available free to elderly people who have a medical condition such as diabetes and ought to be obtainable in their own home. Many types of comfortable slippers and shoes are now available by mail order aimed especially at the elderly and those with foot troubles.

Painful movement

Many elderly people suffer from painful movement to some degree through stiffness or through osteoarthritis and rheumatoid arthritis. Encouraging your Cared-for to move around as much as they are able is a good thing to do. There are many over the counter painkillers available for minor aches and pains, but some elderly people need encouragement to take medication. For more severe pain the doctor can prescribe more efficacious medication but you may still have the problem of compliance. There are several 'memory jogger' pill box devices which you can buy, or you can try making the taking of pills part of the before or after mealtime routine.

Dealing with accidents

Prevention

An elderly lady lived down our street a few doors away from us. We used to see her out and about and knew her well enough to pass the time of day. Coming back from shopping one day I noticed an ambulance outside and my next-door neighbour told me that she had noticed the curtains had not been opened that morning and notified the police. Apparently the old lady had fallen and broken her hip. I was rather ashamed that I had walked by earlier and not even noticed the unopened curtains.

Before considering how to deal with accidents it is worth mentioning again how to prevent them.

Lighting is very important. Replace light bulbs promptly and use the highest wattage that the light shade and fitting allows. Consider free-standing or wall-mounted spotlights near to chairs used for sitting to read, knit etc. Make sure that stair lights can be switched on and off both at the top and the bottom of the stairs and that halls and passage ways are very well lit. A light coloured paint or paper on the walls helps to make the most of the light. Kitchens may need extra 'spot' lighting around food preparation areas and bathrooms near mirrors.

Stairs and hallways need to be kept clear of clutter as much as possible and pale floor coverings help to expose obstacles. A second hand rail can be fitted to most staircases if required. Small rugs should either be taken up or backed with non-slip matting or backing. Loose edges to carpets should be fixed firmly down.

Grab rails can be fitted quite easily by someone reasonably competent in DIY. These are very useful in the bathroom and around front and back entrances, especially if there are any steps to be negotiated. If your Cared-for is very shaky on their feet you might consider a guide rail from sitting room and bedroom to bathroom so that support is available on common routes inside the house.

Calling for help

Alarm call systems can be very useful for your peace of mind. These usually work from a central unit placed at a convenient spot in the house. This unit connects to a telephone line with a microphone so that should your Cared-for press the contact button someone from the call surveillance centre will answer to offer help or re-assurance or to contact you or an alternative named contact. Usually there is also a wrist or neck pendant with a call button which your Cared-for is supposed to wear at all times during the day. The idea behind these alarm call systems is excellent. Unfortunately the system does ask for some measure of compliance from the user and this may be where a problem arises. Many elderly people simply object to wearing the pendant/bracelet, perhaps because it makes them feel 'old' or because they feel that they do not really need it.

My friend arranged an alarm call system for her elderly mother because she was worried in case she might fall and be unable to reach the telephone. Her mother appeared to accept the idea and agreed to pay for it and oversaw its installation quite happily. The only thing was she would never wear the pendant. Whenever my friend went round she would find it lying on a table or a kitchen counter. Her mother said that she always had it nearby but of course if she had fallen she might not have been able to reach it.

Another problem arises if your relative is in the early stages of dementia. They may switch the control box off or unplug it because they have grown used to unplugging electrical items when not in use or simply because they forget what it is there for. If the power is cut off the control centre will normally try to contact the 'named contact' – probably you – and you may find yourself frequently called out at all hours just because the system has been switched off.

> Once when we called round we found a tablecloth had been wrapped around the call unit. After a lot of questioning we worked out that Mother-in-law had pressed the button by mistake and been frightened by the 'disembodied' voice which asked if she was all right. The person at the control centre had tried to tell her how to switch the thing off but she had not understood and had tried to muffle the sound instead.

Many designs of telephone now come with one or more 'one press' buttons which can be programmed to call a particular number. These can be very useful for your Cared-for as you can set them up to dial your number, an alternative number and perhaps the emergency services at one touch. This is a great aid to someone who has poor sight, poor co-ordination or some confusion. You can also obtain telephones with much larger than normal push buttons for those with poor sight or stiff fingers.

If possible ask the nearest neighbours to keep an eye on your Cared-for's house and alert you if they see signs of trouble – un-drawn curtains, lights on all night, milk not taken in. Some neighbours might be prepared to hold a key but you should be careful that both you and your Cared-for are happy about this. In some country areas the local milk delivery person or the postman will keep an eye out for elderly householders.

Keep a good, well-stocked first aid kit on hand in your Cared-for's house in case of accidents. You might also consider going on a First Aid/ First response course in case you discover your Cared-for after an accident and have to wait a while for an ambulance. In some country areas where there might be a long wait for an ambulance even after the emergency services have been called local volunteers provide a 'First response' service where a trained person comes to the house and initiates resuscitation techniques or First Aid procedures whilst you wait for the ambulance. Various groups including some Women's Institutes and The St John Ambulance organise this scheme.

It might also be worth keeping a packed 'emergency bag' or case ready in the house and letting neighbours and friends know where it is or leaving a prominent note of its whereabouts. If your Cared-for does have an accident and is taken to hospital in your absence then there need be no panic about packing nightwear and toilet things for the hospital.

In 'A&E'

If the worst happens and your Cared-for has a fall or an accident and the ambulance is called they will be taken to the nearest hospital with an Accident and Emergency (A&E) unit and this is where they will wait to be assessed. Most A&E units now operate a 'triage' system. People arriving at the unit will be seen by a senior and specially trained nurse who will assess how quickly they need to be seen by a doctor. If you are with your Cared-for you will find that the length of time you have to wait will depend on many things including the seriousness of any injury they may have, the number of other more serious cases awaiting attention, the time of day and the day of the week. Sunday night is still traditionally the worst day/time on which to have an accident requiring care in A&E. While waiting you should not allow your Cared-for to eat or drink unless the nursing staff have told you that you may do so as this may interfere with any anaesthetic they may need.

Waiting in A&E can be very traumatic both for you and your Cared-for. Hospitals differ in both their level of care and their efficiency but the most common complaint from those waiting is of a lack of information. Although the unit looks busy and is crowded with people in uniform of various kinds it may seem a daunting task just to find out what is happening in your individual case. Many units have no obvious central information desk and there appears to be no one to ask what is happening. If you are with an elderly person they will need you to act for them. It is worth remembering that A&E departments have performance 'targets' which they are supposed to maintain in terms of waiting time for patients and treatment. You may not want to appear to be the one 'making a fuss' but once again persistence generally pays off in terms of getting attention. Keep asking and don't be afraid to be assertive. Don't confuse assertive with aggressive. Most hospitals have very strong 'non aggression' policies and they are rightly concerned about any form of aggression or violence shown to staff.

My mother-in-law was taken to hospital following a fall. They suspected that she had a broken hip. She was taken to A&E at 10 am and they began a series of tests and X-rays. My husband and son took it in turns to wait in A&E with her. At 6 pm the hospital told them to go home as she was about to be admitted and to telephone within the hour to find out which ward she would be on. When I telephoned at 9 pm I was horrified to find that she was still waiting in A&E. We went back to the hospital to be with her but still she did not get admitted to the Elderly Care ward until after midnight.

Some hospitals now have a ward where people are admitted temporarily. It may be called the 'Medical assessment ward' or the 'Short stay ward' and it is usually close to the A&E department.

Your Cared-for may be admitted here if the results of tests and X-rays taken in A&E do not define their problem but the staff at the hospital feel that they should not be sent home immediately.

In hospital

If your Cared-for is admitted to the Elderly Care department (you may still think of it under the old term 'Geriatric Care') do not be alarmed. Times have changed and Elderly Care wards are now better staffed and better organised generally than they were in the past. Much of the basic 'hands on' care of patients is now carried out by care assistants (they may have another title depending on the hospital) who have more time to give than the nurses do and most of these are well trained and enjoy working with elderly people. These are the staff who will help your Cared-for wash and dress, who will make them comfortable, chat to them and if necessary help them with meals etc. It is worth you getting to know them. You will also find that careful records are kept not only of medicines and treatment given but of individual care. For example, the care assistants will note that they have washed or helped your Cared-for to shower or washed their hair and so on. Notes about this care are usually kept in a folder near the bed and when you visit you can read these notes and ask any questions about your Cared-for's care or medication.

There will also usually be a leaflet or folder which gives details of the facilities available at the hospital for your Cared-for and of any extra help that you need to provide – for example, in terms of taking away clothing and nightclothes to be washed and returned. It is worth trying to arrange for a member of the family to visit every day not only to cheer your Cared-for but also to keep in careful touch with the level of care provided. If your Cared-for is suffering from dementia and any assessment is to be made by a specialist you can ask to be present and you should definitely make a point of talking to the doctor in charge of your Cared-for's case. The doctor's name will usually be displayed on a sign somewhere near the bed or on a ward plan which is available for you to see. Remember that elderly people even if they are mentally able may be in awe of the doctor and may not react quickly enough to ask relevant questions when they are examined or may not know what questions to ask. If you are not a relative but are the principal carer it is important to make this clear, especially if you have Power of Attorney, as you may otherwise find that you are not given full information.

Leaving hospital

The length of time your relative, or friend, spends in hospital obviously will depend upon the injury or health problem and on how quickly they recover. However, it is unlikely that your Cared-for will be allowed home until some assessment has been made of the home circumstances. Social services will be consulted by the hospital staff if they consider your Cared-for to be a 'vulnerable adult' and they may become involved at this stage even if they have not been before. An occupational therapy assessment of the home may be made to see if your Cared-for can cope on discharge. If you have any doubts about your Cared-for's ability to do so you should voice them to the OT team. If your Cared-for is taken on a visit home for an assessment try to be there as you may notice things that the OT team, however vigilant and well-trained, may not.

My mother was desperate to leave hospital after her stroke. She was taken home for a couple of hours and the OT team assessed to see if she could get around, make a hot drink and had adequate help for getting meals and keeping the house clean. But they didn't notice that Mum could no longer manage to get in and out of bed because her leg was so weak. I don't blame them for this because Mum assured them that she could manage and even said that one of us would always be around to help her. Of course we couldn't be there all the time. Looking back I wish we had been present at the assessment because being used to helping her around the house we might have noticed things they did not.

If your Cared-for could manage at home with just a little extra help to begin with, then it is possible that they might be eligible to receive help from the intermediate care team (terminology differs in different areas) which is available through social services, through the district nursing team or through direct referral from the hospital. The aim of this help is to get people out of hospital and back home sooner than would otherwise be the case. The team will be able to supply care assistants to help your Cared-for with simple everyday personal care including meal preparation up to three times a day for up to 14 days. If you or your Cared-for feel this help is appropriate and it is not offered then make enquiries about it.

An alternative to going straight home is for your Cared-for to be admitted to a local community hospital or to a care/nursing home for a convalescent period. If you feel this is necessary you may have to be quite insistent. Unfortunately beds in community hospitals are in high demand and a place in a care/nursing home may be available only if you are prepared to pay. However, do not be put off if you really feel that you and your Cared-for will not be able to cope at home. Local authorities and social services have what is known as a 'duty of care' and they really must make a proper assessment and offer adequate help. You may find that subtle pressure is put upon you by the hospital who will want to free up their beds as soon as possible and are impatient with 'bed blockers'. They too have targets to meet. But your concern is with the safety and comfort of your Cared-for.

My mother-in-law was admitted to hospital following a fall. At first she seemed to be recovering but then her condition deteriorated and it became obvious that she would not be able to go back home. At this point the hospital began to put a lot of pressure on us to get her moved to a nursing home but it wasn't that easy. We had to check the homes out first and make all the arrangements financially for her. On several occasions when we visited one or other of the doctors would mention that she was taking up a much needed bed but there was no way that we could speed things up. I realise that hospital beds are for acute cases and I feel there should be some kind of 'half way house' temporary arrangement in cases like ours. Of course this was a few years ago and things may have changed now.

Your Cared-for's GP may be very helpful here. He or she will have more knowledge than you of the local facilities for hospital care and they may also be able to put pressure on the hospital if you feel that your Cared-for is being discharged too soon.

When my father-in-law had an accident and was taken to the local A&E department they wanted to discharge him back home that evening. The trouble was that the care package he had been having had been withdrawn as soon as he was taken to hospital (he was under the care of the intermediate care team and obviously they were needed elsewhere) so he would have been sent home without any care. In a bit of a panic I telephoned his doctor and he contacted the hospital. My father-in-law was admitted to hospital overnight until we could get everything sorted out the next day.

When your Cared-for is finally discharged all the relevant people should be informed by the hospital discharge team – for example, the district nursing team, the carers agency, and social services. It is worth you contacting any vital services to be sure that this has happened. You could also try to insist that your relative is not discharged just before a weekend because some of the support teams will not have their full services available then.

Further information – medical conditions

The Stroke Association
Tel: 0845 3033 100
www.stroke.org.uk

British Heart Foundation
Tel: 08450 708070
www.bhf.org.uk

Diabetes UK
Tel: 0845 120 2960
www.diabetes.org.uk

The Alzheimer's Society
UK's leading care and research charity for people with dementia, their families and carers
Tel: 020 7306 0606
www.alzheimers.org.uk

Alzheimer Scotland
Tel: 0808 808 3000 (helpline)
www.alzscot.org

for dementia
Seeks to improve the quality of life for people affected by dementia.
Tel: 020 7874 7210
www.fordementia.org.uk

8

Problems with nutrition

My mother hated cooking even though she had brought up a large family and cooked good meals for us all. When he retired my father took over the cooking and it was something he really enjoyed. However, after he died Mum was faced with cooking again and didn't even have the satisfaction of cooking for others. She often said that she couldn't be bothered to make a meal. She used to go to the lunch club in the sheltered housing complex where she lived and we tried to make sure that she had enough high quality food to prepare simple and quick snacks, sometimes using the microwave to speed things up. However, we couldn't entirely stop her filling up on sweets and chocolates, which she enjoyed, nor to be honest, did we want to. As long as she kept well we thought we'd reached a 'happy medium'.

Generally the nutritional requirements for the older age group are the same as for all adults. The only difference is that there is a smaller energy requirement and very possibly an increase in the need for vitamin D, especially if an elderly person is housebound and therefore does not go outside much. But worry about malnutrition in their elderly relatives or friends is one of the most common concerns expressed by carers.

Sometimes the concern is with becoming overweight. This tends to occur in the young elderly and needs to be addressed by encouraging more activity and keeping to a well balanced diet. Activity tends to decline with age so less energy is expended. The energy requirement for a woman drops from 2200 kilocalories at the age of 18 to 1810 kilocalories at the age of 75 years. It is therefore important that the diet of an overweight elderly person is of a high quality and that so called 'empty calories' obtained from sugar, fat and starchy foods (refined carbohydrates) are kept low.

More often the carer is concerned that their relative or friend is underweight or that their reserves of energy seem low or that they take a long time to fight off minor infections and that these factors may point to inadequate nutrition.

There are various causes of malnutrition in the elderly. One is social isolation. Elderly people living alone may find it too much bother to cook or prepare meals for themselves. They may only eat what they consider gives the least trouble to prepare. It is common to find that tea and biscuits at frequent intervals take the place of a properly prepared full meal. They may frequently say that it doesn't seem worth the trouble of 'cooking for one'.

Another problem is provisioning. It can be difficult to find smaller portions of fresh food when shopping, particularly in supermarkets, which still tend to cater for the 'nuclear family'. Storing excess food is a problem unless there is ample refrigerator and/or freezer space and a good supply of sealable containers for dry goods. Planning and shopping to provide a varied diet may seem onerous. Elderly men in particular may have no idea of the importance of a well balanced diet and even less idea of how to achieve this.

Elderly people who dislike cooking or who do not know how to cook may not prepare adequate meals. It is very easy for them to buy instant 'snack' foods, which are filling and don't need any preparation so that hunger is not a problem to them. The need for a balanced diet may not be obvious because the signs of malnutrition may be insidious and often take a long time to appear.

Elderly people in general may, through lack of stimulus, always eat the same things rather than keeping to a good mixed diet. They can get fixed in their ways and reluctant to try anything different. People in the early stages of dementia may continue to cook the same things over and over again because they are unable to look beyond what comes immediately to mind.

The sense of taste and smell do decrease with increasing age and this may mean that elderly people lose their ability to anticipate and enjoy their food. Smoking and some drugs also affect these senses. Elderly people also secrete less saliva and they may suffer from a difficulty in swallowing (dysphagia). They may also have problems with teeth or dentures. All these physical problems may encourage them to neglect to feed themselves properly.

It is very easy for a carer to go for some time without realising that someone is not eating properly. For one thing your Cared-for might make an effort when you visit to have a meal available. They may fear your censure and lie about what they eat. They may not think it any of your business – after all, it is their life. Someone in the early stages of dementia may not remember whether they have eaten or not recently and may tell you that they have done so as part of the habit of 'confabulation' filling in the gaps in their memory.

As a carer you can help your Cared-for to get the best from their food in the following ways:

Learning to cook

Suggest or arrange cooking lessons if your Cared-for has never been the main cook. Local authorities often have cookery classes which cater for the elderly or those living alone. Your local library will have details of these. But cooking lessons do not have to be formal. Any competent cook can show another person how to make a few simple dishes. This may be an area where younger members of the family who are too busy to assist with the main caring might be able to help. There are also many books available which cater specifically for people 'cooking for one' or focus on simple and quick-to-prepare meals. Some are available in large print (see Further Information, page 139).

Shopping

Ensure enough food is available by making suitable arrangements for shopping. If your Cared-for is able to shop alone you can help by discussing how to plan the shopping around their menus. People who haven't been in the habit of doing the food shopping need guidance, especially on 'store cupboard' items which they may previously have taken for granted as being available at home (think of salt, pepper and bottled sauces, for example). Help your relative or friend to make out their shopping list in advance. If you take your Cared-for shopping yourself than it is still a good idea to make a list in advance but you will also be able to help them shop systematically and to make suggestions about newer and simpler products. If heavy shopping is a problem you can help to arrange home delivery. Some big supermarkets will arrange delivery of the shopping that you have selected in the store. You can also shop on-line from several of the big super-markets and have the goods delivered within a tight (usually two hour) time slot. In small villages the local shops may have infor-mal arrangements to deliver shopping to the elderly or incapaci-tated. You may have to ask as they may not advertise that they do this service. Another useful possibility is the local milk delivery. These days along with the milk many rounds people deliver items such as bread, fruit juice, eggs, potatoes, yoghurt and bottled water. These are staple and/or heavy items which can be delivered directly to your Cared-for's doorstep and cut down on the amount of shopping required.

My mother-in-law had always made her own (delicious) gravy using meat juices from the roast, flour and stock cubes. She complained that she couldn't be bothered to 'go to all that trouble' when just cooking for herself. Therefore she didn't cook meat very often. I introduced her to the various makes of 'gravy granules' which make instant gravy with boiling water. Eventually we found one she liked and she took pleasure in cooking hot meat meals again.

Food storage

Consider the food storage arrangements. The refrigerator should be easy to access and easy to keep clean. Most modern fridge /freezer arrangements house the freezer on the lower level and the fridge at hand height but older single fridges can be quite low and you may find that your Cared-for neglects food items on the lower shelves because of difficulty in bending down. If it is a floor standing model you may be able to raise it to make it easier for your Cared-for to see inside and to reach for items as required. Even if they have never previously owned one, they will find a small freezer very useful. It cuts down on shopping trips and ensures that certain foods stay fresh longer. For example, if your Cared-for uses just a little milk every day most of even the small size cartons will be wasted; small amounts can be frozen in very small containers and moved to the fridge as needed. You can buy very small freezers or combined fridge freezers where the freezing compartment is quite small.

It is also a good idea to check the arrangements for dry food storage. The most accessible cupboards should be kept for foods that are used every day. You can now obtain plastic food containers that are easy to open and easy to wash and keep clean. If your Cared-for has not previously had charge of the kitchen stores show them how to rotatetinned and packet goods and make use of use-by dates. Some of these tips may seem obvious but elderly people often get into a rut in their everyday living arrangements and something as small as encouraging them in re-arranging the food storage cupboards may make their life astonishingly easier.

Make sure that there is a small contingency store of tinned or packet food so that if bad weather prevents shopping or if a carer is prevented from visiting for a couple of days some food is available. Tinned meat stew or tinned fish, tinned potatoes and packets of crackers and digestive biscuits make good standby food. Tinned soup is often popular as it is easily heated up and is hot and comforting. You may periodically have to remind your elderly relative or friend of the store and make sure that they can still prepare it easily. For example, progressive arthritis may make opening tins more and more difficult (see Chapter 5, First Steps for details of appliances and equipment which can help disabled people).

Food preparation

Make sure food preparation is as easy as possible. Modern appliances are a great help. If buying new appliances think about oven timers, automatic ignition on gas cookers and simple to use controls. Consider buying a microwave oven for your Cared-for even if they have not used one before. They can be used to defrost food such as bread which has been stored in the freezer and can speed up the cooking of simple but filling items like jacket potatoes. If your Cared-for has not previously used a microwave oven look for one with simple basic functions. (They will probably be cheaper too.) Encourage your Cared-for to make full use of pre-packed salads, cook-chill dishes and complete 'ready meals'. These are now readily available from supermarkets and via mail-order.

The best thing we did for my father was to buy him a microwave oven. He could cook ready meals, 'bake' jacket potatoes which he ate with baked beans and cheese, heat up soup and defrost a loaf whenever he felt like 'fresh' bread. He always claimed to be unable to cook but enjoyed learning the microwave controls and later bought himself a bigger 'all singing-all dancing' model to experiment with.

Check the stores of food in the fridge and larder of your Cared-for at regular intervals. Partially sighted people may not be able to read 'use by' dates and those who have lost some sense of smell may not recognise 'off' odours from food in the fridge.

Alternatives to self-catering

You could arrange for your Cared-for to attend a 'lunch club' or day centre where a meal is provided once or twice a week. Some elderly people find this a real boon since it means that they do not have to think about and prepare a main meal every day. Others complain about the standard of the food and prefer to manage for themselves. Although an arrangement like this does not solve all the meal preparation problems, it does mean that you can be sure your Cared-for is getting a nutritionally balanced meal at regular intervals. If your Cared-for lives in a sheltered housing complex there is often an associated 'club' or social centre where (usually mid-day) meals are laid on. Your Cared-for will have to pay for the meal of course but this will be offset by the smaller shopping bill.

You and other members of the family, or friends, can take turns to invite your Cared-for round for a meal. There is more detail on cooking or having meals delivered (meals-on-wheels) in Chapter 5, First steps.

Dealing with loss of taste and smell

Some drugs may affect the senses of taste and smell so check with your Cared-for's GP if you think this may be the case. Otherwise, the best way to stimulate these senses is by encouraging your Cared-for to plan, think and talk about food and the menus and dishes which they are going to prepare. If you are serving a meal to your Cared-for take extra care with the presentation. Large portions may put off someone with a small appetite. It is better to offer a smaller portion and second helpings if required. You can also enhance the flavour of dishes by using more sugar or seasoning than you normally would, using stronger flavoured food such as mature cheese, smoked fish and strong pickles and offering extra sauces both savoury and sweet.

Dealing with physical disability

Make sure that food preparation and consumption is as easy as possible by providing your Cared-for with any specially adapted plates, cups or utensils that they may need (see Chapter 5 on aids and appliances). Many 'convenience' foods such as frozen vegetables, boil in the bag rice, and tinned meat and fish are easy to prepare and perfectly nutritious and you could encourage your Cared-for to use them as part of their meal planning. Electric tin openers and mixers and blenders may be useful.

Teeth and mouth problems

Poor teeth or ill-fitting dentures will obviously affect your Cared-for's ability to chew. If possible you should encourage them to have proper dental care at regular intervals. There are dentists who specialise in care of the elderly or in treating reluctant patients and one very good way to find such a dentist is via an internet search (see Further Information, page 140). You can get help with transport problems which make trips to the dentist difficult (see Chapter 4 on Getting about). Many older people find it difficult to clean their teeth effectively. An electric toothbrush can help significantly.

Dysphagia

This is difficulty in swallowing and there are many causes. If your Cared-for has had a stroke or has some disease such as multiple sclerosis than any swallowing problems are likely to be quickly recognised by the medical team looking after them. However, many elderly people do develop dysphagia slowly due perhaps to decreased salivary secretion or some benign condition. If you realise that your Cared-for is having a problem with swallowing arrange for them to see their doctor to exclude any serious or treatable condition. The doctor may refer your Cared-for to a 'swallowing team' attached to the local hospital. Otherwise, a physiotherapist may be able to help. Sometimes there is no treatment which is helpful and you have to help your Cared-for to find ways of making eating, and swallowing pills, easier.

My mother-in-law had real difficulty in swallowing pills and frequently complained of 'something in the throat' but the doctor couldn't find anything wrong and suggested it was a nervous condition. We had to crush all her pills to a powder for her and we used to mix them with a teaspoon of honey. When she went into hospital they didn't realise that she couldn't swallow and nobody checked whether she took her pills. It was only when we found them hidden in her bedside locker that we realised she hadn't been taking them.

High protein drinks can be useful and semi-liquid foods like yoghurt, porridge and milk puddings might be easier to swallow than 'chunky' food. You can puree vegetables and mash potato to make them easier to eat and you can puree fruit and make a 'smoothy'. You may be able to get liquid versions of some drugs instead of pills if you explain to your doctor that your Cared-for has a problem swallowing. Otherwise you can mix powdered pills with a spoonful of something like yoghurt or honey or ice-cream. However, you should check first that this is appropriate. Some pills are specially coated and have to be swallowed whole.

Malnutrition

Clinically evident malnutrition is rare. A sub-clinical deficiency is much more likely and most doctors would agree that it is not always easy to distinguish between the frailty caused by physiological changes in the elderly (loss of muscle tone, for example, and stiffness of movement) and the physical decline which accompanies mild malnutrition. The nutrients generally considered most likely to be deficient are: potassium, folate, vitamin B_{12}, vitamin D, and vitamin C.

As a carer you should be alert and aware of certain indications which might suggest a need for dietary improvement.

Specific signs of nutritional deficiency are:

- Weight loss and loss of energy – this may indicate insufficient food is being eaten or food is not being absorbed properly.
- Excessive thirst, urinary infections, sunken eyes – may indicate inadequate fluid intake.
- Weakness and tiredness, sore gums, slow healing of wounds – may indicate low vitamin C intake.
- Fractures, bone pain – may indicate low vitamin D intake, though osteoporosis should be considered first.
- Anaemia, tiredness, inflamed tongue – may indicate low intake of folic acid

- Tiredness, headaches, brittle spoon shaped nails, sore tongue – may indicate lack of iron in the diet.

Generalised signs that might suggest attention should be paid to the diet:
- Weight loss, complaints of tiredness and weakness
- Dry lips, painful mouth, sores (similar to cold sores) on lips and around mouth
- Dry, unhealthy look to the skin, and/or sore skin
- Constipation
- Ravenous appetite when given a meal indicating a possible neglect to prepare own meals.

If you suspect that symptoms are related to nutritional deficiency be sure to mention it to the GP. A doctor may be looking for medical reasons for any symptoms and unless they have regular experience in looking after the elderly may not think about their nutritional status. You can ask for your Cared-for to be referred to a dietician if you are really worried but you can do many simple things yourself to help improve their diet.

We had a very nasty experience when arriving to visit my mother-in-law one day. She had had a severe nose-bleed and been unable to clean up properly. The place was a thorough mess but she didn't seem to have knocked her nose or done anything to cause the bleed. When we consulted the doctor he could find nothing wrong but suggested we look at her diet. It turned out that although she had been making meals she never cooked vegetables (too much trouble) or ate any fruit. We don't know if this was the cause of the nose-bleed but we brought her some vitamin pills and made her take one each day and made sure that there was plenty of fruit juice open in the fridge for her to use.

How to help

1. Ensure your Cared-for takes a daily multi-vitamin pill. There are many to choose from but check to ensure that the one you choose includes a good dose of vitamin C.

2. Ensure that your Cared-for drinks a daily glass of fruit juice (not fruit drink or squash). Good helpings of fresh fruit and vegetables would also be useful. From the vitamin and fibre point of view fruit and vegetables are interchangeable so if your Cared-for does not like vegetables (many elderly men profess to disliking them) then fruit would be a good substitute and vice versa. Sometimes advice about 'five a day' leaves out the fact that either fruit or vegetables are appropriate. The advantage of fruit is that most fruits can be eaten without cooking. Of course many vegetables can also be eaten raw but elderly people may find them difficult to chew in the raw state (see mouth and teeth problems, page 134). You could make sure that a bowl of fresh fruit is always available and regularly replenished. You could also make sure to include salad in the diet.

3. Suggest a 'nightcap' of hot milk or milky drink such as cocoa. It is better if this is made with milk rather than from one of the 'instant' hot chocolate drinks because these are usually made with dried skimmed milk. Whole milk is better for an underweight person.

4. If bad teeth or ill-fitting dentures or sore mouth discourage your Cared-for from eating fruit or vegetables, puree some and mix with ice-cream, or gravy in the case of vegetables, to be eaten with the next meal.

5. Suggest 'instant' porridge oats for breakfast, quickly cooked in the microwave. Again this will be better if made with milk or if milk is added.

6. Leave tasty sandwiches in the fridge prepared with tinned fish, cheese or egg and salad. Sandwiches can be a good meal for someone living alone and because they need no preparation your Cared-for may eat more. Eggs are particularly good in the diet as they are easy to prepare, can be cooked in many different ways and are very nutritious. They are also tolerated well by those with a poor digestion for meat. It is a myth that they raise cholesterol levels in the blood.

7. Take your Cared-for out for a meal occasionally. This may re-kindle their interest in food and you will gain an insight into what foods they like to eat.

8. Give supplement drinks inbetween meals. They come in many flavours and are usually made with milk. They are obtainable in many supermarkets and in pharmacies. You should not have to go to a health-food store to get them. Check the labels as some have a much higher sugar content than others. Sometimes it may be possible to get them on prescription. Ask the district nurse about this.

Special needs

In general, doctors recommend that a good varied diet provides all the nutrients a person needs, but any acute illness in the elderly may be accompanied by a loss of appetite and they may take longer to recover than younger people. Some maladies that are more common in older people, such as leg ulcers and pressure sores, take longer to heal if the diet is poor. If your Cared-for suffers from an acute or chronic condition then you might want to consider giving a food supplement. Vitamin C, zinc and the B vitamins are all easily available in pill form and you might consider adding these to your Cared-for's daily diet. If they find it difficult to take conventional pills these supplements can be found as easy-to-take 'chewable' jellied sweets or as a syrup. Be careful about excessive vitamin C. It will do no real harm but may cause diarrhoea in high doses. If your Cared-for does not get out into the sun and open air much you might also like to consider suggesting they take Vitamin D either in pill form or as cod-liver oil.

There has recently been research which indicates that taking a combination of pure EPA (eicosapentaenoic acid) and virgin evening primrose oil is effective in the treatment of dementia, arresting the development of symptoms even in very severely affected patients. (The supplement used in the most recent trial was VegEPA, which contains these two essential fatty acids.) For further details about this research see page 141.

Some literature on nutritional problems in old age and on dementia suggests that various traditional medicines may be useful. The most commonly mentioned are Ginkgo (for memory problems and peripheral artery disease), Ginseng (as a general pick-me-up), and Glucosamine (for cartilage problems). Generally, none of these therapies will do any harm if your Cared-for takes them in the recommended dosage and they may do some good, but Gingko should be stopped well before your Cared-for undergoes surgery as it can lead to haemorrhage. (For guidance on the safe use of traditional herbal medicines see details of the book by L Karalliedde in the list below.)

Further information – nutrition

Simple cookery
Marion Cunningham
How to Boil an Egg: ... And 184 Other Simple Recipes for One
Elliott Right Way Books 1997

Wiltshire Farm Foods
Deliver frozen ready meals to your home
www.wiltshirefarmfoods.com
tel; 0800 773 773

British Dental Association
To search for a dentist who specialises in elderly or reluctant patients
www.bda-dentistry.org

Igennus
To order vegEPA
Tel: 0845 1300 424
http://vegepa.com

Karalliedde L, Fitzpatrick R (2006) *Traditional herbal medicines – a guide to their safe use*. Hammersmith Press, London.

Essential fatty acids and dementia

Kavanagh T, Lonergan PE, Lynch MA. Eicosapentaenoic acid and gamma-linolenic acid increase hippocampal concentrations of IL-4 and IL-10 and abrogate lipopolysaccharide-induced inhibition of long-term potentiation. *Prostaglandins Leukotrienes and Essential Fatty Acids* 2004. 70: 391-397.

Puri BK, Leavitt BR, Hayden MR, Ross CA, Rosenblatt A, Greenamyre JT, Hersch S, Vaddadi KS, Sword A, Horrobin DF, Manku M, Murck H. Ethyl-EPA in Huntington disease: a double-blind, randomized, placebo-controlled trial. *Neurology* 2005. 65: 286-292.

Puri BK, Bydder GM, Counsell SJ, Corridan BJ, Richardson AJ, Hajnal JV, Appel C, McKee HM, Vaddadi KS, Horrobin DF. MRI and neuropsychological improvement in Huntington disease following ethyl-EPA treatment. *Neuroreport* 2002. 13: 123-126.

9

Dealing with dementia

One of the most difficult things to admit to oneself is that that a loved one is becoming demented even if all the signs are obvious to others. Dementia is also one of the most difficult things to deal with when caring for a relative, friend or neighbour.

As noted in Chapter 7, Recognizing medical conditions, there are two recognized types of dementia in the elderly, although both can be present at once. Alzheimer's disease is the one most people have heard of and it accounts for approximately sixty per cent of cases. Vascular dementia (often associated with a series of strokes) accounts for about fifteen to twenty per cent. Dementia can also result from a number of other, much more rare diseases and conditions and a dementia-like condition can result from certain nutritional deficiencies. If your Cared-for has been diagnosed with one of the other primary causes of dementia such as Huntington's disease then it is likely you are already well aware of what this means.

Some medical conditions can have symptoms similar to those of dementia, which is why a definitive diagnosis is essential if you suspect it in your Cared-for.

Dementia is progressive and gets worse over time. Symptoms are mild in the early stages and the carer can do a lot to help. Chapter 7 on Recognising medical conditions suggests signs which might indicate dementia. Although a diagnosis of dementia may make families or friends decide that their Cared-for should move to a care or nursing home this is not always the best answer in the early stages. Studies have shown that people with mild to moderate dementia go downhill less quickly when they are kept in familiar surroundings and cared for by people they know. This chapter suggests ways in which you, the carer, can help the dementia sufferer and also ways in which you can make life easier for yourself and anyone else involved in their care.

Memory loss/forgetfulness

It is difficult to comprehend the 'memory loss' of dementia. It is not like the normal 'where did I put my keys?' lapses which we all suffer from occasionally. People who suffer from dementia might forget where they live, for example, which is why you often hear stories of elderly people 'wandering'.

> We used often to see an elderly neighbour walking the streets near us and would exclaim at how active he was and how good it was that he kept fit by taking walks. Then one day he approached us when we were walking by and said 'Excuse me, can you tell me where I live?' It appeared that he would regularly forget the way home and keep walking around until something sparked off his memory and he found his way back. It was an eye-opener for us as he had always appeared quite alert when we greeted him. We had had no idea that he was so confused.

The memory loss appears to be spasmodic at first so that the sufferer might forget the way home one day but be perfectly all right the next. People with dementia may actually forget what some objects are or what their purpose is. As you would expect, items which are used most often are more likely to be remembered than those which are not.

I remember my sheer amazement when I first realised the extent of my mother's memory loss. I asked her for the spare car keys (she was a non-driver) and because I knew her habits suggested that she look first in her handbag. She went through each item in her handbag one by one asking me, 'Is this the car key?' even about items like business cards or her comb. It was one of the most upsetting episodes in our relationship.

Many people with dementia forget the day or the date. They may ask you frequently what day or date it is or alternatively they may argue with you and flatly deny the facts. When you say that it is Saturday for example, they may insist that it is Monday.

Some people with dementia will deny events that have clearly occurred. This is because they have no memory of them. They will perhaps claim that you haven't visited them for several days when you have actually called every day.

In the early stages much can be done to help memory lapses. But be prepared for many repetitions and the re-covering of old ground. For example, you might accompany your Cared-for on a local walk and point out one or two memorable landmarks which might help them find their way home. 'See, there is the post-office. Now we only have a few houses and then we get to your home'. Or, 'When you see that big oak tree you will know that you are nearly home'. Your Cared-for is quite likely to say something to the effect that 'I know that', but it is worth persevering. The constant repetition and pointing out of landmarks might save them wandering many miles one day.

A useful idea is to buy a large wall calendar and encourage your Cared-for to cross off the date every evening before bed, or every morning after breakfast. Then if they forget the date they can check the calendar. This will only work if you are able to instil the habit of crossing off the date. Another idea is to show your Cared-for where the day and date are printed on the daily newspaper. They can always check the date that way, but again you will need to instil the habit of looking there.

You can encourage remembrance of events by gentle reminders. 'I came to see you yesterday, remember, and we ate some chocolate éclairs for tea.' Or, 'We went out together yesterday and did the shopping. Remember you bought those bananas.' Material reminders around the house will often, when pointed out, trigger the lost memory.

Simple card games like 'snap', and 'pairs' are a help to the memory too, as are games like scrabble and noughts-and-crosses, and doing jig-saws.

Confusing time

People suffering from either form of dementia may become confused about the time of day. Strangely this does not usually mean that they lose the ability to read the time from a clock. Indeed, if asked they may tell you the time and take a pride in being able to do so. But the actual concept of the hour of the day means nothing to them. Even the fact that it is dark or daylight may not convince them that it is night or day.

My mother-in-law went through a period of ringing us up in the early hours of the morning and announcing that she was just cooking dinner – or had just got dressed – or was waiting to go shopping. No amount of telling on our part would convince her

---

that it was night or that she should go back to bed. She would say 'I don't want to go to bed. I'm just making myself some chicken and chips' or some other bizarre (to us) reply. Conversely, sometimes the assistant from the care agency would call at mid-day and mother-in-law would refuse to answer the door because she had just gone to bed.

It can help here to link an event with a common occurrence rather than naming a time. For example, you could say, 'We are going shopping after such-and-such a television programme', or 'I have to go home after we have had tea'. Telephoning or wandering the streets at night are more difficult to deal with. You can try explaining that if it is dark they should not go out, but if the curtains are closed they may not realise that it is dark. You can also be as short as possible when answering a night-time telephone call but it may not have an effect.

Neglecting personal care

Over time a person with dementia may begin to neglect their personal needs such as the need to wash, to change their clothes and to eat properly. They may forget how to dress themselves and begin wearing a strange assortment of garments.

My father stopped bathing and shaving. At first he would wash and shave if I took him to the bathroom and insisted, but then he started resisting. I discovered that if I started the activity – put the razor into his hand and turned him towards the mirror he would carry on. It seemed that he was just not able to initiate things – as if he didn't know how to start.

Some activities will be continued more than others and there does not seem to be a standard pattern. For example, your Cared-for may still undress and carefully hang clothes on hangers but not be able to find fresh clothes in the wardrobe without prompting. Or they may change their clothes but hide the soiled garments rather than putting them in the laundry basket.

There are many ways you can help your relative or friend to cope and in the early stages helping them to manage as much as possible by themselves will increase their self esteem as well as saving you time and trouble.

It is best not to ask someone with dementia if, for example, they would like a bath or a wash. They will very likely say no. Instead lead them to the bath after you have filled it and begin to help them remove their clothing if necessary. Or walk them to the shower, turn it on and ask them which soap they would like to use.

Remember that bathing/showering every day is not absolutely necessary for cleanliness, though incontinence of course can make this more of an issue. Daily bathing or showering is a relatively modern habit and a thorough wash will do just as well. If certain parts of the body such as between the legs, under the arms and the face and hands are washed regularly an all over bath or shower can be delayed until convenient.

If necessary help to initiate the action of washing and then step back and see if your Cared-for can continue alone.

Routines such as washing hair, which involve a little more effort and which are not necessarily done every day, may be neglected sooner than daily routines. Your Cared-for may claim that their hair does not need washing or perhaps even that they have already washed it. Again, it is good to remember that previous standards do not need to apply. Hair can be washed about once a fortnight provided it is thoroughly brushed/combed each day. Some people find leaning forward over a basin uncomfortable or frightening. You could try washing hair in the shower or letting your Cared-for sit in a chair and lean backwards over the basin. A large towel wrapped around them will mean that wet clothes do not become a problem. Some people with dementia will resist washing hair themselves but see a visit to the hairdresser as a treat so you could arrange a regular appointment.

Washing feet and cutting toe nails is another chore often avoided, particularly if your Cared-for has trouble bending forwards. It is possible to buy sponges on long sticks for use when washing the feet but those with dementia may not be able to learn how to use such aids. Suggest a weekly 'beauty treatment' which could involve washing the feet, applying foot cream and trimming the nails. If your Cared-for can afford it, you could arrange a regular visit from a chiropodist. (Chiropodists will provide free nail care to elderly persons who have another medical condition – such as diabetes.)

When tackling problems with dressing try laying out clean clothes in the order in which they will be put on. Avoid complicated fastenings which may be difficult for rheumatic hands. However, many people with dementia can remember familiar actions such as doing up buttons and zips, for a long time. Make sure that clothing is loose and comfortable and take notice if your Cared-for shows an aversion for a particular garment. In such a case do not insist on them wearing it. You can purchase clothing which is easier to put on such as pull on trousers and skirts with elasticated waists, but your Cared-for may prefer the type of clothing they are used to.

Refusal to recognise the needs of others

People with dementia are often unable to understand that others have needs as well as themselves. They may begin to appear selfish and demanding. If you are caring for two elderly people living together and one of the partnership begins to develop dementia you may feel the need to defend the non-demented partner to the other. 'Dad isn't being unkind, Mum – he just can't manage to help you cook'. This is probably a waste of time. If possible it is best to ignore complaints and to support the non-demented partner in doing likewise. Taking the non-demented partner out regularly or arranging for the one with dementia to attend a day centre will give much needed breaks.

If you are caring for an elderly person living alone and they begin to develop dementia they may start to complain that you or others are neglecting them even when this is untrue. Again there is very little point in defending yourself or others. Try instead to maintain your sense of balance. They cannot help themselves and do not understand the stress that they are causing. You in turn should *not* feel guilty about your own feelings of annoyance because you are doing the best you can to care for them. You may also feel guilty because you lose your temper sometimes, but do remember the sufferer will forget your cross words sooner than you do. It is very useful to 'sound off' sometimes to a friend who you can trust. It may be best to avoid using another family member for this purpose as emotions are likely to be already very mixed in the family. You may also find the support of a local carers group valuable. Try to give yourself regular respite time and holidays from caring if at all possible (see Chapter 13, Caring for the carer).

Fears and delusions

Irrational fears may be an early sign of dementia. For example, your Cared-for may begin to keep doors locked or put furniture in front of external doors to 'stop anyone getting in', which could of course prove dangerous if they needed emergency help. They may begin to refuse to use one room in the house or to allow you to enter that room. They may claim that an innocent person like the postman is bothering them in some way. Your re-assurance may help for a time but because of the memory lapses which are common with dementia they may not remember your explanations for long. Insisting that they enter a room or leave a door open may make your Cared-for very nervous and cause a bad reaction. Increase their sense of security by allowing them to keep doors or windows closed unless it is necessary to open them. (You can open windows to air the house whilst you are present and close them when you leave, allowing your Cared-for to check they are closed, perhaps). Make sure that you have keys to the house in case your Cared-for refuses to answer the front door. If your Cared-for does begin to refuse to open the door you should make sure that any door chain is removed or you may find yourself locked out even with your keys. Sometimes arranging a special 'ringing code' will ensure that they answer the telephone if you call. Of course, you may have to repeat instructions for this dozens of times. Sometimes people with dementia develop a fear that seems completely inexplicable, such as a fear of a piece of furniture or of a particular flower or scent.

My mother-in-law was afraid to sleep in the bed after my father-in-law died. At first she slept in the spare room but later she avoided going to bed at all, preferring to spend the night in her reclining armchair. It took a while before we realised this was happening; only piecing together snippets of conversation and 'clues' from the cleaning lady made us realise. It became clear that she had had 'an accident' and wet the bed once. This was not a regular occurrence but it had frightened her enough to put her off using the bed. I brought a mattress cover and spent a long time showing it to her and explaining that this would protect the mattress if anything of the sort happened again. Eventually she did sleep in the bed again but she occasionally reverted to sleeping in the chair if anything had upset her.

The simplest thing to do, if reassurance doesn't work, is to allow the fear without agreeing with it. In other words, avoid buying that particular flower or using that scent or move the piece of furniture to an out-of-way place. But do not admit that the fear is rational.

People with dementia may appear to have delusions, but it is often difficult to tell if these are real delusions or are just the result of 'confabulation'. Your Cared-for may say that they have received a visit from someone when you know this to be untrue. It may be that they are under the delusion that someone has visited but it may just be that they came upon a cup of tea which they had forgotten about and have 'filled in' the memory lapse by 'confabulating' a story about someone coming to tea. Sometimes the stories are very strange and often they concern long lost relatives visiting. People with dementia seem to lose later memories before earlier ones and so may insist that a deceased son, daughter or husband is still alive and even that they are frequent callers. There does appear to be a tendency for those with short-term memory loss to 'fill in the gaps' when recalling something and this may account for some 'delusions'.

Difficulty with conversation and loss of speech

This manifests itself in a variety of different ways depending on the individual. One major difficulty seems to be an inability to tell you something in a way that makes sense even though the ability to talk is unimpaired. For example, your Cared-for may try to explain that someone has telephoned them. 'The bell rang....Sally....very loud......coming today....yesterday.' Or they may substitute a word which has associations with what they are trying to say, 'We went out to the grass' (garden).

This type of difficulty calls for a lot of patience from the carer. You may have to spend a lot of time trying to unravel the meaning from a jumble of phrases, especially if your Cared-for is upset about something and you feel that you really need to get to the bottom of what it is. Over time you may learn to understand the 'word associations' your relative or friend uses but they may not remain consistent since dementia is progressive.

One idea is to try to get your Cared-for to lead you to where they want to go or to point to what they mean. For example they might point to the telephone if relaying news of a telephone call. It might help you to write down key words as you 'unravel' what the story is so that you keep to the point and don't get led astray by irrelevancies. In the example above about the telephone, the phrase 'very loud' is not significant but 'coming today' probably is. It may take several attempts for you to understand and your Cared-for may just give up the effort if you press too hard. You could also try to relax them and pick up the thread again later by referring to the matter in a gentle tone. Anxiety tends to confuse someone with dementia and they are likely to be put off if you convey your own worry to them or if you try to press or 'browbeat' them into explanations. Remember too that certain concepts may be conveyed correctly even though the words are wrong. Your Cared-for might say 'park' instead of garden or 'taxi' instead of 'bus', but the inherent meaning is there.

My mother said one day, 'My cousin came to see me yesterday – my girl cousin'. Well, to our knowledge Mum had no cousin left alive, but after I thought about it a little I asked her, ' Do you mean that your sister came to see you? Jeannie?' She was delighted that I had understood. She knew it was a relative but the only word for a relation she could recall at that moment was cousin.

Another major difficulty may be in your Cared-for's understanding of speech. They may not respond at all when you ask them a question. This is because they are unable to make sense of what you are asking. A frequent problem is when the person with dementia responds 'No' to every question. They may not understand what is being asked, but somehow they seem to sense that a question often involves something they don't want to make the effort to do. Or they may sense that replying 'No' often makes the questioner give up and stop bothering them. Occasionally a person with dementia answers 'Yes' to every question instead, or 'Yes' and 'No' at random. The best way around this is not to ask questions unless really necessary. Instead of 'Would you like to go into the garden?' say, 'Let's go into the garden now', perhaps taking their arm and leading them, gently. Instead of 'Would you like a cup of tea?' say, 'I'll make you a cup of tea now'.

When you have to explain something use short sentences and simple language.

'We are going for a walk now,' *not*,

' I thought we'd go out for a walk after you've eaten your lunch. It's really quite cold so you'll need your coat but I can fetch it later.'

It is also worth reinforcing your words with actions – fetching the walking stick if you are suggesting a walk or offering the plate of cake when asking if they want a cake. It also helps to use body language: 'Is your foot hurting?' (touching the foot and looking concerned).

Sometimes a person with dementia retains a social veneer which enables them to maintain a conversation but if you carry the conversation beyond the simple 'social' level they are unable to respond. However, the social veneer is very valuable and can be helpful to the self-respect of the person with dementia.

When I first employed a professional carer to help look after my sister I had trouble convincing them on the first visit that there was anything wrong. My sister made the tea and sat talking with us, even making voluntary remarks about the weather or a TV programme she liked to watch. It was only as the carer began to visit regularly that she realised that my sister would use the same phrases on every occasion. It was always 'a lovely day', or she 'loved the gardening programme'.

Even when having a conversation is difficult, the effort of doing so can be helpful to your relative or friend. Talking about familiar things and naming common objects helps to retain speech and understanding as long as possible. You could, for example, name things as you go along in as natural a way as possible.

'We'll put the sandwiches on this plate and the cake on this plate. If you carry the sandwiches in, I will bring the cake.'

Looking at photographs and watching video tapes of past events is very helpful both as an aid to memory and as an aid to speech.

' Oh look, there is Andy kicking the ball. He looks happy.'

'Do you remember when that rose bush was against the wall there? It was a lovely colour.'

Another element of not understanding speech is the loss of the ability to understand the written word. Surprisingly many people with dementia can still read perfectly well; they just cannot understand what they are reading.

When my mother was in hospital they used to bring round the menu cards for her to choose her meals. She would proudly read out to me 'Breakfast; choose two; orange juice, porridge, toast....', but she was quite unable to choose what she wanted unless I translated by asking her in simple terms, 'Would you like toast for breakfast?'

Often someone with dementia might seem to be reading a magazine you have provided, but if you talk about any of the articles it becomes clear that they do not understand what they have read.

Incontinence

Incontinence is discussed in Chapter 7, on recognising medical conditions. When people suffer from dementia they frequently become incontinent and it is often listed by carers as one of the most difficult things to deal with. At first a person with mild dementia seems to understand and to be upset and embarrassed by incontinence, and at this stage you will probably find that they try to hide 'accidents'. Later they may appear to ignore or even to be unaware of it. When someone is only mildly demented it may be possible to explain to them the use of incontinence pads and pants and what to do with their wet or soiled clothes, but you should still be ready for odd lapses of memory.

I began to notice a smell of urine on my visits to my mother. She denied any problem and always said that she couldn't smell anything herself. She didn't like me poking around the house so it wasn't until one day when my brother had taken her out shopping that I got the chance to have a good look around. I found dozens of pieces of underwear, towels and old rags stuffed behind the radiators. She had obviously cleaned up after her 'accidents' and then tried to hide the 'evidence'. Luckily she was still able to understand how to cope after I had explained to her what to do and provided her with proper incontinence clothing. I did find that she had the odd lapse but the smell would alert me and I would simply go through the instructions with her again. She was able to just about cope until her death.

It is a waste of time, as well as unkind, to get annoyed when someone with dementia suffers from incontinence. They really cannot help their 'accidents'. However, it is worth having them checked over by the doctor because urinary infections can sometimes cause temporary incontinence, which will resolve when the infection clears up. It is also worth investing in clothes with simple fastenings which are washable. Sometimes incontinence is simply the result of not getting to the lavatory in time. In cases like this, taking your Cared-for to the toilet regularly may help to avoid accidents.

Frequently the onset of incontinence is the 'last straw' that causes families, or friends, to contemplate helping their Cared-for move to a nursing home. It can be some consolation in these circumstances to remind yourself that your Cared-for will at least be kept clean, dry and comfortable as nursing home staff are used to dealing with the problem and have the facilities and equipment to cope.

Mental Health Act

Patients with dementia can, in principle, be detained under the Mental Health Act 1983 of England and Wales. In Scotland, Wales and Northern Ireland the legislation is differently named. For example, in Scotland there are the Adults with Incapacity (Scotland) Act 2000 and the Mental Health (Scotland) Bill 2002. Northern Ireland has The Mental Health (Northern Ireland) Order 1986, while the Republic of Ireland has The Irish Mental Health Act 2001.

In England and Wales, dangerousness is an important reason for the compulsory detention of an individual with dementia under the Mental Health Act 1983. This dangerousness may be to others or to oneself.

Dangerousness to others might occur if, for example, a

patient loses their normal social inhibitions. The definition of 'dangerousness' is not confined to threats or physical violence towards others. It may refer to things like indecent exposure or even sexual molestation.

Dangerousness to oneself can cover such things as forgetting to switch off electrical or gas appliances so causing a risk of fire, trying to have a bath or shower in water that is too hot with a risk of scalding, or being unable to feed oneself properly, keep sufficiently warm in winter or keep clean and avoid infections.

Admission to hospital, under mental health legislation, might only need to be on a temporary basis, while measures are taken to circumvent such problems – for example, automatic electrical switches can be fitted which switch off cookers, irons, etc. after a limited time-period, and regular assistance can be provided to help the individual to bathe, shower, feed and keep clean.

Further information – dementia

The Alzheimer's Society
UK's leading care and research charity for people with dementia, their families and carers
www.alzheimers.org.uk
Tel: 020 7306 0606

Alzheimer Scotland
www.alzscot.org
Tel: 0808 808 3000 (helpline)

for dementia
Seeks to improve the quality of life for people affected by dementia through training of specialist nurses and carers.
www.fordementia.org.uk
Tel: 020 7874 7210

Incontinence Products
www.dryforlife.co.uk
Tel:0800 180 4325

Mental Health Act
The final section of this chapter developed from a contribution by Professor Basant K Puri. See also:
Puri, BK (2005) Old age. In: BK Puri, RA Brown, HJ McKee and IH Treasaden. *Mental Health Law: A Practical Guide.* Hodder Arnold, London,

10

Care agencies and professional carers

Mum could manage the routine housework even though she couldn't see very well, but we needed to get some regular help for 'difficult' jobs such as cleaning the windows, vacuuming under the bed, and trimming the hedges in the garden. She could afford to pay and I thought it would be a simple matter to find a handy person who would come in regularly. But I was amazed to find how particular the agencies were. Some would do only 'light housework' and some would do internal chores but nothing in the garden. In the end we had to have a mix of options and my sister and I took over the difficult vacuuming by taking it in turns once each week.

Sooner or later you or the person for whom you are caring may begin to consider the need for professional carers to help on a regular basis. It may be that you live too far away to carry out your caring duties on a daily basis. Or perhaps you have a job which prevents you being able to carry out much physical daily care. It may be that the needs of your Cared-for have developed beyond what you and other family members or friends are able to provide for.

In theory, local authority social services departments are responsible for arranging services to help older and disabled people stay in their own homes. Many people believe that they *have* to get this sort of help through social services or that social services will recommend a care agency. In fact, you are perfectly at liberty to make your own private arrangements and you can contact a care agency direct without involving social services. Although the local authority social services department may furnish you with a list of approved or inspected agencies, they will not usually make a specific recommendation.

Getting help through social services

If you or the person you care for decide to arrange help via social services this is the procedure. The first step towards arranging home care services is for you or your Cared-for to contact your local council social services department for an assessment of needs to be undertaken. This assessment is sometimes known as a **Community Care assessment**. The social services department is supposed to react in a timely manner according to the urgency involved. If, for example, you have suddenly fallen ill and your relative needs immediate help, then the Duty Officer in the local department ought to be able to call on someone to provide help immediately. On the other hand, if you are just making enquiries about what help might be needed at a future date, your need will be assessed as much less urgent. Be aware, however, that each department reacts differently according to its efficiency, and the calls that it already has on its resources as well as on its assessment of the urgency of the case. If you do not feel that you are getting a service that is fast enough, be prepared to keep calling and keep insisting that your need is urgent.

The assessment process will examine the needs of the person you care for and how they can be met. During an assessment your

Cared-for (and you, if you choose to be present, and you should arrange this if you possibly can) will be asked questions about their circumstances, the situations and activities they find difficult and any support that they receive from family, friends, neighbours and the community in which they live. The assessment process should involve other professionals such as the GP or the district nurse or anyone who has been closely connected with providing care. The social worker doing the assessment should provide you with information about what support is available locally, so that you can make a choice about how your Cared-for's needs should be met. This information may be as simple as telling you to call in a local cleaning agency (which social services will employ on your behalf), or suggesting you check your local Yellow Pages for a window cleaner. On the other hand, it may point you to useful local services that can provide for your Cared-for's specific needs.

At the end of the assessment process you and/or your Cared-for should be provided with a clearly written statement declaring what you and your Cared-for need, how these needs will be met and which organisations or individuals can be involved in meeting those needs together with their contact details. This statement is called the **care plan**.

At this point there can also be an assessment of your Cared-for's finances, which will look at both income and capital savings to see how much they can afford to pay towards services provided by the local council. There are wide variations in how much is charged. However, government guidance states that charges must be 'reasonable' and must not cause undue financial hardship. You can get further details about charges from various websites or telephone helplines (see Chapter 3 Entitlements, benefits and how to apply for them). If your Cared-for is too poor to make any contribution to the cost of care services but is clearly in need of them the local authority *may* fund these. However, there is virtually no direct provision these days of what used to be known as 'home help'. In cases where the local authority will fund help they will contract with a private agency to provide the care and pay the agency direct. 'Home helps' directly employed by the local authority are a thing of the past.

But councils also have a duty to offer the choice of **direct payments** to all individuals who have been assessed as needing services and who meet certain criteria. The Direct Payments Scheme means that your Cared-for can directly receive funds to 'employ' their own support, rather than having services directly supplied by the council.

Generally speaking, if your Cared-for can afford to do so they will have to pay something towards professional caring services whether you arrange these via social services or privately. Agency fees are usually quoted on an hourly basis and include administration charges. The general rule seems to be that the actual carer receives between one third and one half of the fee you pay to the agency.

Arranging professional carers privately

It is neither as quick nor as simple to call in a professional caring agency as you may think. Therefore it is a good idea to begin your research as soon as you start to think their services might be needed, even if it appears that that date is some time in the future.

This chapter gives some general advice about where to start when researching professional care and some information that will help to save time and trouble during the actual process of arranging care.

There are various different types of agency and before contacting any it is good to make a list of what specific help you and your Cared-for require. This helps you to narrow down the list of agency contacts and to give specific information to the agency when you do make the contact.

Broadly, professional caring falls into four main areas:

Nursing care

It is possible to obtain private nursing care in your own home and there are agencies who specialise in hiring out nurses for this purpose. Such care is usually very expensive and if your relative is sick enough to require nursing care at home it is very possible that it is available through the National Health Service (NHS) so make careful investigations first, unless you specifically want to use private care. Your local NHS provider can supply help with:

- continence advice and equipment
- chiropody
- occupational therapy
- physiotherapy
- medical equipment, such as wheelchairs and special beds

Care for patients with a specific illness such as cancer or multiple sclerosis can also sometimes be available through the NHS. To find out what is available in your area approach your Cared-for's GP, or better still the District Nursing Service.

Professional agency nurses are usually very specific about the services that they will and will not provide and the agencies through which you obtain this care will explain this to you. In general, do not expect a professional nurse to deal with personal care such as bathing or helping with dressing or with any form of housework or cooking.

Cleaning and household duties

There are agencies that will provide people to tackle cleaning and housework but if this is the only sort of help your Cared-for needs you may prefer to make a private arrangement with an individual cleaner. Agency fees tend to be very high for this type of work. However, hiring through an agency will ensure that you get continuous cover during holiday times or sickness and the agency will take care of PAYE and National Insurance matters for you.

They will also follow up the references of their workers and you may feel that it is worth paying for this convenience. A cleaning agency will usually do an initial survey of your needs and will provide a written document stating what services will be provided. You may be surprised to discover that private cleaning services, whether through an individual or an agency, can be quite particular about what they will and will not do. Some cleaning services will not make beds or change bed linen, for example. Many cleaners refuse to do 'heavy work' such as cleaning windows. The unfortunate thing is that frail elderly people can often cope with routine daily chores and it is with the 'heavy' work that they need the help.

My parents already had a cleaner whom they trusted and who seemed willing and competent. So when it became a problem for Mum to change the duvet cover I thought it would be simple to ask the cleaner to extend her duties to include this. I was amazed when she told me that she 'did not do beds'.

Companionship

You can actually pay for 'companionship' - that is, having a more able-bodied person around most of the time - and some agencies specialise in this type of service. You might choose this option if your Cared-for is housebound or has an otherwise restricted social life and if you and the rest of the family or other friends are unable to supply all they need to combat loneliness or other social needs. These paid companions will usually do light shopping and collect prescriptions or library books. They will also take your Cared-for on outings or stay at home with them and keep them company, playing card games, chatting and being available if your Cared-for is nervous when tradesmen call. Some agencies will provide carers who give a companionship service in combination with cleaning or personal care. Again, you will need to make careful enquiries.

Personal care

Carers from agencies who provide this service will help with things like getting in and out of bed, bathing and washing, and dressing, as well as preparing meals, shopping and cleaning. Depending upon your needs, some agencies will also provide staff who will give medicines, stoke solid-fuel stoves, defrost freezers and turn their hand to whatever needs doing.

Choosing an agency

Once you have narrowed down exactly which services you require you can begin researching care agencies. There are a number of options when it comes to finding the right one.

- You may be able to get details of approved private agencies from your local social services department. Ask for the company registration department. Remember that they are not usually allowed to recommend a specific agency.
- You may get a recommendation from a friend or relative. This can be very helpful as you will be able to get an idea of the standard of care received and also of the quality of administrative handling (see below).
- You can use the internet or the local telephone directory and find care agencies in your area. At first there will seem to be a bewildering number available to help you with care. In fact you may find that your choices are much more limited. The web pages or telephone book may have a long list of names but often all three types of caring agency are lumped together under a generic term such as 'Nursing and Care Agencies', meaning that you will first

have to sift the list to extract only those that provide the services you require. To increase the difficulty, many agencies do not specify in their advertisements what type of care they provide. You may have to make several initial investigatory calls just to narrow your search to those who will provide what you require.

- The UK Home Care Association (contact details are at the end of the Chapter) can give you details of home care providers who follow their code of practice.

Practicalities

Find an agency that works in your area.

Many advertise that they give a country-wide service (they are part of a chain); others operate only locally. Here again you may have to speak to them to pin down availability. The initial advertisement might indicate that the agency supplies services throughout your county but when enquiring you may find that they cannot supply your particular area because they do not have carers either living in or willing to travel there. Of course, there is more likely to be a problem in rural areas and especially if you need carers to come to an isolated village or house.

Plan the times and days you need help.

You need to consider whether the person you care for needs help every day (with washing and dressing, for example) or only once or twice a week (for cleaning and housework) or perhaps at more irregular intervals (hedge cutting, window cleaning) and you need to consider whether some of the help needed can be supplied by family or friends. For example, you may consider asking for a professional carer to come in on weekdays while the family can provide cover at weekends and on bank holidays. This is very important because weekend and holiday cover is likely to be much more expensive and also because (you may be surprised to discover) the agency may simply not be able to cover at holiday times. It depends on how many of their staff are willing to work the 'unsocial hours'. Be aware of this because the agency will not necessarily tell you this in advance of your entering into a contract with them.

> The agency we used said that they could cover 365 days of the year if we required it. But when our usual 'days' occurred over holiday time we had to re-book ahead to say that we wanted cover then. In addition we occasionally got letters to say that they actually could not provide cover on certain days. For example, one Christmas when we had planned to go out on Boxing day we received an apologetic letter just before Christmas saying that they couldn't provide cover that day so we had to change our plans at the last minute.

Discuss how the care will be provided.

The agency may try to ensure in so far as it is possible that it is always the same person who provides care and that someone else will only be sent in case of sickness and holiday. They may, however, not be able to agree to this. They may have part-time workers and shift workers and job-share workers and the person coming to provide care may be different on different days and at different times. This is especially likely if your Cared-for needs care at different times of the day – for example, in the morning with getting out of bed and dressed and in the evening with getting undressed and back into bed. Some elderly people whilst accepting the need for regular help will be upset with the seemingly impersonal nature of this type of provision. If your Cared-for suffers from dementia they may be afraid of strangers and bewildered by different carers appearing at different times and you would have to take this into consideration.

Find out what the carer will do.

It has already been mentioned that some agencies only deal with one aspect of care. Even when agencies say that they will tackle multiple tasks you need to clarify what is not allowed. For example, a carer may be allowed to give medicine provided you have left it out with the correct dosage (say, two pills in a container to be taken at midday) but may not be permitted to decide for themselves when to give a dose. Medicine is a difficult area. Some agencies will say that their carers can 'encourage' the person in their care to take medicine but not actually hand it to them. A carer may be prepared to heat up a ready meal but not to cook food from scratch. You will also have to bear in mind the time factor. Only so much can be achieved in a set amount of time. In one hour a carer could heat up a meal, wash up and quickly dust around but they couldn't also vacuum the house and make the bed. Usually the agency will give you guidance on this. Different agencies also have different rules about whether carers can take charge of money to buy shopping, for example. Most have a rule that carers cannot accept ex-gratia payments.

Check up on administrative details.

All agencies must produce a statement of purpose and a service user's guide which details at the minimum:

- The aims and objectives of the agency and the type of services provided, including specialist services
- The people for whom the service is provided
- An overview of the process for the delivery of care and support
- Key contract terms and conditions: whether you will be issued with a contract by the agency and what arrangements have to be made for unusual occurrences
- The complaints procedure
- The Quality Assurance process

- Specific information on key policies and procedures. For example, you would want to ask whether, if your Cared-for goes on holiday or into hospital, a 'retainer' needs to be paid to the agency
- How to contact the Commission for Social Care Inspection (CSCI), social services, health care authorities and the General Social Services Council (GSCC)
- The hours of operation and details of insurance cover.

This is the time to find out whether you or the person you care for will be invoiced and how often. If you have power of attorney you should specify that all invoices come to you. You should also ask about written care plans, and whether notes are left by the carer on each visit. Don't be misled into believing that an ultra-efficient administrative package means that the care is better or alternatively that late invoices mean a bad standard of care. The administration and the caring usually rest with two different departments of the agency and efficiency in one may not mean the best service in the other.

What to expect from the agency

After making initial contact and establishing that you want to take things further with the agency the next step will be a visit by a **care manager**. If you employ a care worker from an agency without having an assessment by the council, the agency must carry out a full assessment of your care needs. At this visit they may also carry out what is know as a 'risk assessment' on your Cared-for's home and circumstances. Even though professional carers carry out some tasks which other people find distasteful or difficult there are certain rules about what they are allowed to do and the agency still has a duty regarding health and safety towards their employees. The care manager will want to look around the home and note unsafe equipment or problems which might prevent the carer giving the required service. They will also want to talk to your Cared-for about the service they are going to receive. Only after this visit and after receiving and signing the care agency contract will you be able to arrange a date for the professional carers to begin visiting your Cared-for.

All this can take some time – several weeks perhaps, and if social services are being involved it might take even longer. This is why you need to think about your Cared-for's need for professional care well in advance if you can. Also, once you have a system of care set up you may be surprised to find that to extend or improve the care plan may take time. It is not simply a matter of calling the care agency and saying that now you would like the carer to call three times a week instead of twice. Agencies have their rotas to arrange and are often short of staff prepared to do the tasks required. Again it is worth trying to foresee what might be needed a few months down the line and planning for it early on.

If you are employing the agency directly you should be provided with a written contract within seven days of the start of the service. The agency must have a confidentiality policy, which they must provide to the client (you or your Cared-for) and which must detail how they will hold and use personal data. There must also be clear, written policies and procedures covering how staff administer and assist with medication.

Even if you or the person you care for have arranged private care without involving social services you will not always be allowed to retain that privacy. Nearly all care agencies have strong links with the local authority social services departments and can and do report to these departments about individual clients if they think it necessary. If a case is reported to them the local social services have what is known as a 'duty of care' and must make further enquiries.

We had begun to think that Mum needed further care from the agency on a daily basis and had arranged a family meeting to discuss this. The day before the meeting I was astonished to be called by the social services department who told me that the agency had reported to them that they were concerned about my mother's care and that they wished to set up a meeting with me. I was amazed that the agency had approached social services without talking to one of us first but when I took this up with the Care Manager she was quite unapologetic and refused to see that her behaviour was at all improper. To make matters worse, when we did agree the need for daily care the same agency then said they didn't have enough staff to provide it!

Once you have set things up with the care agency your day-to-day relationship, and that of the person you care for, will then be with the carer or carers who provide the actual services you have negotiated. It goes without saying that individual carers vary in how willing they are to go 'beyond the call of duty' and also in how well they manage to get on with your relative or friend. It is a good idea to have written list of what you want the carer to do, whether on a daily or an occasional basis. For example, if you expect them to provide a lunch-time meal and to make the bed each day but you also require a variety of jobs (say, wiping out the fridge, vacuuming one room, cleaning the bathroom) on a regular but not daily basis it is best to ensure that a list is made, agreed to and kept available. Then, if your regular carer is replaced by someone else due to sickness or holiday the replacement carer knows just what to do on any given day.

The first carer my mother-in-law had was absolutely wonderful. She carried out all the tasks we gave her and filled in her allotted time by doing odd jobs like tidying the freezer or polishing the bookshelves. She got on well with mother-in-law as well. One day when my mother-in-law had an acute attack of her arthritis and was unable even to get out of her chair to answer the door the carer climbed into the house through a window to look after her! Unfortunately this carer had to retire due to illness and although the next carer was pleasant and did what we wanted she made it plain that she couldn't be expected to do anything extra.

If the person you care for dislikes having a professional carer, is a little awkward or suffers from dementia, then you may find there is a problem when the carer needs to gain entry to the house. Your Cared-for may refuse to answer the door or may turn the carer away. Generally, this means that you (as the main contact) will be telephoned. Perhaps you will have to go round to the house to persuade your Cared-for to let the carer in. On the other hand, where the carer works to a strict schedule with other clients to visit they may have to cancel their visit on that day. Agencies vary in their attitude to these episodes. Some may not charge you but others will maintain that their employee was ready and willing to do the agreed service and that payment must be made regardless. Not all professional carers are prepared to hold a front door key but most are happy to take a key from a coded 'keysafe' outside the building and to let themselves in. You may need to resort to this if the person you care for needs help in getting out of bed (see the Further Information section).

Both the actual carers and the caring agency are usually used to awkward clients, to elderly people who are perhaps grumpy and difficult and to clients suffering from dementia. They will often work hard to maintain their relationship with the client and the family in difficult circumstances. However, most carers have a schedule to keep and agencies have a business to run. It is important to understand their point of view when it comes to difficulties with your Cared-for. However, the agency will have policies about certain things and you or the person you care for are at liberty to ask them about these in relation to such things as knocking/ringing the bell and speaking out before entering the home, who keeps a set of keys and where they are kept, the confidentiality of entry codes if you use a key safe, for example, and what alternative arrangements they have for gaining entry if the usual arrangements fall down, securing the house when they leave it and what they will do if your Cared-for has an accident.

Generally, the care agency will provide a timesheet or 'log' which the professional carer will complete on each visit. This is a very valuable piece of information for you since it will inform you about such matters as what your Cared-for has been given to eat, how they appeared physically to the carer, what work the carer has carried out and any problems which they wish to bring to your attention. Where you have been forced to engage a professional carer because you are prevented yourself (perhaps because you have a job or you live at a distance) from seeing your Cared-for on a daily basis the log provides a useful tool for keeping in touch. You can also compare the daily log with the care plan which has been provided by the agency and point up any problems or potential difficulties early on.

If you do encounter any problems, then obviously the first thing to do is to raise them with the agency manager or the care manager who deals with your Cared-for's case. Then follow the agency's own complaints procedure. If your Cared-for suffers from dementia or is muddled in their mind then make absolutely sure of your facts first. You can try following the tips in Chapter 9 Dealing with dementia, in order to establish the truth as nearly as you can. There are two elements here which are sometimes difficult to reconcile. You want your Cared-for to be treated with care and concern for their dignity and the agency carer is in a position of power if your Cared-for is weak or helpless or unable to communicate. On the other hand, as pointed up in the chapter on dementia, sufferers may 'confabulate' or fill in memory gaps with statements of what they think happened. However, it must be said that if you or your Cared-for has real doubts about the care they are receiving, it may be better to switch to another agency if there is one available. [Comment: always check how long a notice period you have with an agency? Not sure where this should go..]

Help through the NHS

In some cases, and usually in emergencies, caring teams are also provided through the NHS. The work these teams do is sometimes referred to as **intermediate care**. The name varies depending upon which area you live in. The intermediate care team can provide up to two weeks' care up to three times per day in the case of a 'crisis at home'. This means, for example, if the person you care for needs this level of care but you or they are unable to arrange your own provision immediately. It might apply if your relative or friend was being discharged from hospital following an accident or illness or it might apply if the normal carer was ill and unable to supply the current level of care. The team is also able to cover up to three nights' 'night sitting' if your Cared-for is unable to be left alone all night. These teams consist of multi-disciplinary support workers trained for up to one year in various areas of caring and the standard of care given is generally excellent. The teams are accessible via the district nursing team, the hospital from which discharge is being arranged or social services and your Cared-for's needs may be referred through any of these depending on circumstances. Unfortunately it is true to say that this help is not always offered as a matter of course when required, so be prepared to ask for it if you need it and to be gently insistent about your need.

Further information – professional care

UK Home Care Association
Tel: 020 8288 1551
www.ukhca.co.uk

SUPRA UK
Outdoor key safes to hold the door key to your Cared-for's
house securely
Tel: 08700 539723
www.keysafe.co.uk

Services provided by your local authority will be listed in your
local library and on the individual local authority websites.

11

Choosing a care or nursing home

The question is bound to arise eventually of whether the time has come when it would be more appropriate for your elderly relative or friend to move into an environment where they would be able to receive a higher level of care. Many people have to make a decision about a care home in a crisis, perhaps after a fall or illness, or the death of a partner. Looking back they often wish they'd had longer to look around. So if you think your Cared-for might need a care home in the future, it's a good idea to do some planning sooner rather than later. This would also give your Cared-for time to get used to the idea. This may be much easier for them if initially the suggestion is put forward simply as something that 'might happen sometime in the future'. You may find it useful to refer to Chapter 1 on Managing change when you and your Cared-for tackle the task of moving into a residential home.

If your Cared-for lives alone then you and they may begin to feel that there is a need for a more constant presence in their lives. If you are already living with your Cared-for and providing live-in care then it may be that you feel you can no longer cope or are no longer able to provide the level of care required. You may consider the possibility of your Cared-for moving into warden-controlled accommodation. However, you do need to be aware that in most accommodation of this kind the warden is supposed to be there in case of emergency only. In some types of complexes the warden may, as a matter of goodwill, also run small errands for the residents and carry out small services for them, but in others there is strict 'call service' operating, which means that unless your Cared-for actually calls for help (or in some cases fails to answer the routine 'check up' telephone call that the warden makes) no follow up will be made. If you are afraid that your Cared-for may simply need help in an emergency only (perhaps following a fall) then this may be sufficient for your purposes. However, for most of us the big change comes when we and others have to consider the need for accommodation where help is always on hand as and when it is required.

Types of residential accomodation

Residential accommodation for the elderly falls into three categories. There are 'Care Homes', 'Nursing Homes' and 'Care/Nursing Homes for the Elderly Mentally Infirm' (EMI). Your Cared-for may need one type of accommodation now and to move on to another later in life.

Care homes

Care homes are the ones we tend to think of as 'old people's homes'. This accommodation is meant for elderly, reasonably fit people who can look after themselves to a certain extent in everyday matters. These homes are not meant for elderly people who need 'nursing care'. If your Cared-for lived in this type of home they would have a room or apartment which would probably be cleaned for them, and communal lounges and other facilities would be provided. Meals would also be provided, probably in a communal dining room (although some homes provide a kind of 'room service' for meals). The benefit of this type of home is that the burden of providing for everyday living in the form of cooking, cleaning and associated shopping is lifted from the residents, they have company should they wish for it and help is at hand if an emergency arises. Many such homes provide social activities on site and such useful facilities as a visiting library, film service, and small shop for necessities such as toiletries, or stamps. These homes do not provide for elderly people who need nursing care every day although some may have a visiting doctor or nursing service. Usually these homes can provide some help with 'personal care' if your relative needs help with washing and dressing.

Nursing homes

Nursing homes are a separate category of home. They have a trained nurse on hand at all times and they will provide for people who are less able to manage their own personal care. They are also able to provide nursing for chronic conditions such as leg ulcers, pressure sores and certain disabilities and conditions (for example, diabetes) where the intervention of nursing care might be required periodically. Different staff in these homes will deal not only with routine cleaning and domestic chores (as in a care home) but will also provide help with washing, dressing, moving about, and eating and drinking if required.

Dual registered homes

Dual registered homes offer both residential and nursing care. They may be the right choice if you think the level of care your relative or friend needs may change in the future, or for couples who each need different levels of care. Dual registered homes will normally be registered for specific numbers of nursing beds and residential beds, and availability will depend upon the home's assessment of your Cared-for's needs and the availability of an appropriate bed. It is possible to find registered homes where all the types of care are provided in different buildings on the same site so that if your relative or friend starts off needing simple nursing care but later suffers from dementia, for example, they can simply move to another building with the minimum of disruption.

EMI homes

These homes provide for those elderly who are mentally infirm (usually dementia sufferers) who may or may not be able to manage some of their own personal care but who in any case need a close level of supervision either to stop them 'wandering' to prevent them harming themselves or to help them with everyday living. Some residential care homes and some nursing homes also offer places to dementia sufferers.

The state only provides free residential care for the least well off. It is therefore quite likely that your relative or friend will have to pay at least some of the costs of accommodation and personal care in a residential or nursing home. The amount the state (actually the local authority of the area in which your friend or relative lives) pays depends upon the capital that your Cared-for has. The capital amount taken into consideration is different in England, Scotland and Wales. If your Cared-for has capital below a set amount (currently in England £12,500, in Scotland £11,750 and in Wales £14,750), then the State will fund the full cost of residential accommodation. Some payment will be made if your Cared-for's capital is above the minimum up to a maximum. If they have capital over this maximum they will have to pay the full cost of accommodation. If their capital falls below the upper amount whilst they are in a care home, then they will become eligible for help from the state. If your friend or relative wants a more expensive home than the local authority is willing to pay for, you are allowed to arrange a 'third party contribution' from another source. Your Cared-for's home would be included in their assets only if they live alone. In addition, the local authority will disregard the value of their home for 12 weeks after their admission to permanent nursing or residential care. This will mean that if, without the house, the value of their accountable assets falls below the threshold they will have a breathing space to make plans, or sell the house. Your Cared-for will be expected to use all their income – including any pension, benefits, and so on – to fund care. However, a small weekly amount can be kept as spending money.

Nursing care is defined as care that must be provided by a registered nurse. An assessment needs to be done to see whether this level of care is needed. If it is, it will be funded by the state. The payment depends on whether nursing needs are assessed as low, medium or high. This contribution applies whether care is funded privately or by the local authority. If your Cared-for is paying their own fees, they will still have to pay for accommodation and personal care (such as help with dressing or bathing).

In Scotland there is a flat rate contribution per week for personal care, plus an amount per week for those assessed as needing nursing care. In Wales there is a flat rate contribution per week towards nursing care. Quite often the individual nursing home will help you to make the claim for nursing care contributions and once you and your Cared-for have decided on a home then it is worth you discussing this with the administrative staff there.

My mother was already in receipt of an attendance allowance. Once we had settled on a nursing home I thought I would have to go through a lot more form-filling to try to claim nursing fees but the matron of the home told me that she would attend to that. Apparently 'nursing care needs' cover a variety of things. For example, the fact that my mother had a pressure sore meant that she qualified for some nursing. I was really glad to be able to let the staff at the home deal with the claim for us.

Paying for care is a complex subject, and everyone's situation is different. You should seek advice about your Cared-for's individual case. Organizations which offer specialist advice are listed at the end of this chapter and in the reference section. Immediate care insurance may be suitable if you are currently considering helping your Cared-for to move into a care home. It involves paying a single large sum at the time you and your Cared-for decide residential care is needed. The cost is based on the length of time the insurer thinks care will be needed, and the level of care required. While the cost can seem a large amount, it should provide a fixed payment for as long as your friend or relative needs care, and can protect the rest of their assets. The payments are tax-free if they are generally made directly to a care home and are portable if you and your Cared-for decide to move to a different home. Further information on this subject can be found in Chapter 3 on Financial matters.

Drawing up a short-list

You and your Cared-for will wish to take time to research the availability of places and to view individual homes. To begin your search it may be useful to speak to friends and relatives, for their recommendations, as well as your Cared-for's GP or the District Nurse. Your local social services department should be able to provide a list of registered homes in your area; otherwise you could search the internet or research in the local telephone directory. A useful idea would be for you and your Cared-for (and any other members of the family who might be involved) to first make a list of any criteria which are important to you. For example, you might want a home which is near enough for you to visit your Cared-for frequently. Your Cared-for might have their own ideas about room sizes, the standard of common facilities (dining room, lounge) or the availability of en-suite toilet and bathing facilities. Perhaps your Cared-for enjoys being outdoors and the size and type of grounds are a consideration.

> When we started looking for a residential nursing home my mother-in-law was already suffering from dementia and unable to make a decision about where she wanted to live. We were looking locally and because she had been a keen gardener we were zeroing in on places with pleasant communal gardens. But in the event my sister-in-law decided that she wanted her mother to live nearer to where she lived and she did her own research, eventually finding a really nice nursing home two hours away from where we lived. It seemed strange not to be able to visit as frequently as we had been used to but we had to agree that the nursing home chosen was just right.

Every residential home, whether run by the local authority or privately, is inspected annually by the **Care Commission**. Registration of the home is subject to certain standards and these are the criteria which govern each inspection. After the annual inspection a report is made and these reports are lodged in the local public library. Many homes also publish the results of the report on their website if they have one and some local authorities may publish these reports on the local authority website. The report includes information on the number of beds, the immediate surrounding area, the number and qualifications of the staff and the facilities provided. It also includes the fee rates. Once you have produced a list of homes to consider, then the annual report is probably a good place to start to reduce your list to a shortlist of places you and your Cared-for would like to view.

If your Cared-for will be paying all the care home's fees, you and they can contact homes directly. Once you have found a home you like, the home will make an assessment of your needs, so that they can be sure they can offer you the right kind of care. If your Cared-for needs nursing care, for example, the home will have to be able to supply this.

If the local authority is being asked to help with all or part of the fees, you should speak first to your Cared-for's GP and the local social services department. They will carry out an assessment of your needs, and produce a report called a **care plan** that outlines the care, including any nursing care, they think your Cared-for needs. If your local authority is assisting with funding, it doesn't mean you have to choose one of their homes. You can still do your own research locally and you can request any home that accepts residents funded by the local authority. However, the local authority will want to be sure that the home is suitable for your needs and doesn't cost more than it would usually pay for that type of care. If a more expensive home is wanted than the authority is willing to pay for, you or your Cared-for will be allowed to 'top up' their contribution from another source. You may be surprised to know that the majority of care homes in the UK are owned by the independent sector, and that 70 per cent of residents have their fees paid partly or wholly by their local authority.

An initial telephone call to each home on your short-list will help to clarify some points and to reduce your shortlist still further. Simply assessing whether the phone is answered promptly, whether the person answering is helpful and assured, whether your questions are answered clearly and fully and whether a visit is offered or further information (for example, referral to a website or an offer of a brochure) provided, will help you to decide whether to follow up with a visit. Be wary if the person you speak to suggests that you only visit at a certain time or on a certain day. Of course you will want to time your visit for when the Matron or some other person with knowledge can be on hand to help you, but a well-run home should have nothing to hide from a chance visitor.

If your Cared-for has some specific criteria of their own when considering a care/nursing home, then in some respects you will have a ready made short-list of homes. If, for example, your Cared-for is a Roman Catholic and wants a home run by a religious order, or if Jewish Kosher cookery is important to them, or if they will not consider going into a home where they are not allowed to keep their pet with them then the choice will be restricted. The choice will also be restricted by the type of home required as detailed above. You choice might further be restricted by the scale of fees that your Cared-for can afford or which the Local Authority is prepared to pay. However, after taking these things into consideration you will probably have a list of three or four homes which you will wish to visit.

Taking a look

What things you look for on your visit will depend upon your Cared-for's wishes and circumstances. It is possible to obtain standard lists of 'things to look for' and 'questions to ask' but these will of course be generic in nature and it is more useful to decide about what the most important things are for your friend or relative personally and then add on a wish list or a list of things they would be unwilling to accept in a new home. Listed below are some factors you might want to consider and some suggestions as to how you can decide what fits your own and your Cared-for's particular criteria.

Locality

Is the home in the locality or community your Cared-for wants? They may want to be near to where you live (or another family member) or conveniently situated to visit friends or to havefriends and family visit them. So the accessibility of the home may be very important: whether it is on a bus route, or near a railway station, or whether it has ample car parking. Your Cared-for may want to visit local amenities such as shops, churches or pubs. If your Cared-for has enjoyed a good social life they will want to be able to continue this as far as possible, so they may, for example, want to be near the church they have attended, the club they belong to or the shops they prefer to visit. They may want to live in a home where one or more of their friends already live.

Immediate surroundings

Most homes have some sort of garden but you should consider the surroundings as carefully as you would if your Cared-for were moving into a private home. For example, your Cared-for may not want a home situated too near a busy and noisy main road, they may want to have good views of gardens and countryside from the windows, or alternatively they may want somewhere where they can 'watch the world go about its business' even if they cannot go out much. In such a case a home with windows looking onto the street might be preferred. If there is a communal garden, then what is it like? If your Cared-for is or has been a keen gardener they might think interesting shrubs and plants and the chance to help with some small garden tasks are more important than clipped grass and a tidy appearance. If they particularly enjoy being outside then it is worth checking if it is easy to go out into the gardens and whether there are comfortable seats in the garden and smooth paths for walking.

Accommodation

Remember that this is to be your Cared-for's home. Naturally the communal areas should be well decorated, bright and cheerful and clean. The home should smell fresh and there should be no unpleasant odours. It might be important to your Cared-for that they can have their own room decorated to their own taste so this is something you may want to check. You will also want to check if they can bring items of their own furniture if this is important to them, as well as pictures, ornaments and other items. Some homes allow pets and this may be a major criteria for your Cared-for. Some homes will allow residents to bring their own curtains, rugs and bedding and again this may be a very important factor. You should also check on some things that you may think would be taken for granted. For example, is it possible for the heating to be adjusted in different rooms and can your Cared-for easily open and close the windows in their room. Everyone feels temperature differently and having control over his or her own 'micro-climate' might be a major factor for your Cared-for. Your Cared-for might like to have their own telephone line and you can check whether this will be allowed, though mobile phones have made this less of an issue. Most homes are now happy for residents to have their own television in their room but perhaps your Cared-for prefers the radio or to listen to music? You may want to see if the facilities would be available for this.

The Matron of the home we were viewing had two rooms available. She was rather worried about showing us one of them, explaining that the occupant had recently died and had never been a very tidy person. She didn't want us to get the wrong impression from an untidy room. In fact I was more impressed that the previous occupant had been allowed to be untidy – in other words, at least her room was her personal space and she could relax in it in her own way. It was this respect for the individual that made us choose this home in the end.

Equipment

If your Cared-for needs help with daily living then you should pay special heed to the facilities available. There should be enough bathrooms and they should have proper toilet aids and items such as bath hoists, accessible showers and emergency call facilities. Many homes now offer en-suite toilet and washing facilities and this may be a major factor for your Care-for. Some people particularly dislike using communal washing and bathing areas. Some homes still offer shared rooms and this too may not suit your Cared-for. Most nursing homes have a call system in each room, but you may want to check if this is easy for your Cared-for to use and perhaps see for yourself how quickly it is answered. If your relative or friend needs help to move around you might want to check for handrails in passages and communal rooms and to see if rolator trolleys or walking frames are allowed and if the passages and doorways are wide enough to accommodate them. If your Cared-for particularly wants a ground-floor room because of difficulty using stairs, this may be a major factor on your checklist. Homes will naturally have stair-lifts or elevators where these are required, but your Cared-for may not be able or willing to use these on their own and a room on an upper floor would therefore not suit them at all.

Communal areas

You and your relative or friend may want to think about the security of the home. Although visiting should be allowed at any time, there should be a way of checking visitors in and doors onto the street or non-enclosed gardens ought to be securely fastened to prevent undesirable or unauthorised people wandering into the home. Your Cared-for may be concerned about the security of their own possessions so you may wish to query whether they can lock their rooms when they leave them or whether there are facilities to secure cash and valuables.

Some homes have a dining room, but others serve residents' meals in their rooms or in the residents' communal lounge. Some offer a mix of both. You may want to enquire whether your relative or friend can choose where to eat and whether they can invite visitors to eat a meal with them either in the dining room or in their own room provided notice is given. (Your Cared-for would expect to pay for any guests, of course) Being able to invite guests for a meal may make all the difference to the acceptance of the idea of a residential home being really a 'home'.

Not all homes can offer two lounges, but the old fashioned picture of a roomful of elderly people blankly gazing at a TV screen might fill you with horror. If there is only one lounge then you might like to enquire whether the television is switched on continually or how and when it is decided what will be viewed. Of course, your Cared-for can always escape to their own room but not everyone wants to spend the day in one room. What other communal rooms are there? Is there a bar, for instance, or a games room or a library? Which of these might be important to your Cared-for? If being able to smoke (or choosing not be exposed to other people's smoke) is important then you will want to enquire about the smoking policy – that is, whether there are smoking and non-smoking areas and whether smoking is allowed in residents' rooms.

Facilities and entertainment

How important these are depends upon how active your relative or friend is and how independent. If your Cared-for enjoys an active social life in the community and intends to continue this, then they may not be too concerned about 'in-house' entertainment. In this case, discuss and examine the ease with which residents can plan outings or opt out of meals and whether any transport is organised by the home to get to local events. If your Cared-for is suffering from dementia then some things, like music therapy or memory therapy, say, might be more important than outings and films. So you would want to know whether these types of therapy are organised and what facilities are available to stimulate the minds of dementia sufferers. If your Cared-for is mentally active but has physical problems in getting about, then the most important facilities might for example, be visiting entertainment (films and live shows), library book supplies, visits by hairdressers, facilities for people with hearing/visual difficulties, or availability of facilities to carry out any hobbies or interests.

Whilst viewing homes for my mother-in-law who suffered from dementia my sister-in-law visited one home which made a great display of the many 'therapies' available. At first she was very impressed but during the visit it later became clear that residents were more or less forced to take part in the activities whether they wanted to or not on the grounds that they were unable to decide for themselves what would be 'good for them'. My sister-in-law made a throw-away remark that the number of activities might leave the residents quite exhausted and received a very frosty response!

Some details about facilities need checking as a matter of course. For example, you could ask to see the laundry room and enquire whether laundry of personal belongings and bed linen is charged as extra. Sometimes room cleaning is also charged as extra, and you might like to enquire whether the rooms are cleaned on a daily or weekly basis. Your Cared-for may want to continue to be seen by their own GP and so you would want to check whether this is possible. Depending upon the area it may be that your Cared-for's GP would not be able to visit them in their new home. Similarly, it can be very useful to know what arrangements are made for visits by or to chiropodists, physiotherapists, opticians and dentists. Don't assume that there is a standard procedure.

Catering

If your friend or relative has special dietary needs then, of course, this would be at the head of your list of questions. If they need religious dietary considerations (no meat on Friday and Abstinence days, or Kosher cooking, for example), then your choice of home might be limited. But even if this is not the case you and your Cared-for might like to know the standard of the cooking, whether a visitor can be invited to join a meal, what sort of choice of menu there is and whether meals must be taken in a particular room or whether your Cared-for can eat in their own room if they wish. You could also enquire whether alcohol is allowed and can be ordered or bought for your friend or relative if this is important to them. It could be worth organising your visit to coincide with a meal-time to get your own ideas of the quality of food served, the serving arrangements, and the state of the food when it actually reaches the residents.

Staffing and daily concerns

The published inspection report should give details of staff qual-ifications. Some demands for training may seem excessive to you and you may be more concerned as to whether the staff seem kind and caring and whether other residents seem cheerful and calm in their presence. There are now rules about the number of staff who have to have received a certain level of training, but training does not guarantee kindness and consideration nor does it ensure that those caring for your friend or relative will maintain their dignity and take extra trouble to accommodate their individual wishes. It can be useful to enquire about the number of staff on duty including those on duty at night. A nursing home should have a trained nurse on duty at all times. You may also like to make enquiries about the use of 'bank staff' and 'agency staff'. Most homes will have to make use of these at times of staff holiday or illness but it will obviously be more pleasant for your Cared-for if they are generally looked after by the same people who will have a chance to get to know them. These days most homes have a personal 'care plan' for each resident and you can enquire about these and ask whether you will be able to see the notes made about your Cared-for's care during your visits.

> When my son and I visited the nursing home where my father eventually lived we had to wait for a short time in the hallway until the Matron was available to see us. We were sitting outside one of the rooms and the cleaner was working inside. What impressed me was the manner in which she chatted to the elderly lady whose room it was. The old lady was clearly unable to answer but the cleaner kept up a really pleasant and cheerful conversation and took such care when moving the old lady's possessions about that we gained a very good impression straight away.

It is also useful to make enquiries about whether there are set times for getting up and going to bed and whether a resident can request a bath or shower when it suits them. Of course, in a busy home some structure has to be maintained but it could be very annoying for your friend or relative if they are always got out of bed first because their room is at the end of a particular corridor! As already mentioned, you should enquire about the visiting policy and be very wary of homes where there is much restriction on visiting. The best homes allow visiting at any hour of the day or night, although of course they should monitor the admission of visitors. If your Cared-for is active they may want to help prepare meals or clean around the home or even arrange flowers and set tables etc. In this case, find out whether such help is welcomed. Not everyone wants to be waited on hand and foot.

Fees

Finally you will want to make enquiries about payments. You should be careful to ascertain what is included in the standard weekly or monthly charge – for example, does the charge include laundry, chiropody or hairdressing? Some homes make an extra charge for toiletries such as soap and shampoo or for extra drinks and refreshments. If extra charges are made for such items, when and how are they billed? Check how often fees are reviewed. It can be galling to be quoted a fee only for it to be increased within a month. It is easy to forget to ask such details as whether fees are payable in advance, whether they can be paid by direct debit and, especially, what happens to fees paid in advance if your Cared-for leaves the home mid-month or dies. If you hold power of attorney or otherwise manage your friend or relative's financial affairs, then you need to ensure that the bills will be sent correctly to you.

After the move

My mother was suffering from mild dementia when she moved to a care home. I used to visit once a week and became a bit concerned because she said that they had stew for dinner every day. So I changed my routine and visited on several occasions around meal times. Of course, I found that the menu was good and varied. Because I had always visited on the same day and her

> memory was short she could only remember what she had eaten that day. Sometimes it was goulash, sometimes curry, sometimes casseroled beef but to her it was always 'stew'

Once your friend or relative is settled in the home you will be able to plan your visits. Hopefully you have chosen a home which allows unrestricted visiting and it is a good idea to vary the times and days of your visits or to plan with other friends or family so that visits are spread over different days and times. It is always useful to see how the home runs at different times of the day and to get an idea of the routine. Visits are important for your Cared-for who will look forward to seeing you and to the variation in their day. Visits are also important for you because they enable you to see how your friend or relative is cared for. In the early days your friend or relative may have several grumbles but these are likely to be the result of settling in to a new home and a new routine. If you have serious worries about any aspect of care or behaviour of the staff always follow them up.

- Always listen carefully if your Cared-for complains. If they suffer from dementia it is even more important to try to understand their concerns. (Some tips about unravelling confused speech are given in Chapter 9 on dementia.)
- Try if possible to get the name of the member or members of staff concerned.
- Always carry your concerns to the Matron or Care Home Manager in person.
- Ask for a follow-up interview to hear how your concerns have been addressed.
- Keep bringing your concerns forward even if you are treated as a nuisance. (Your Cared-for needs your help.)

- Keep written notes of any conversations you have about such concerns, making sure you write them up as soon as possible after they've taken place.
- If you are part of a family or group of friends try to maintain a united front when handling any concerns/complaints.

I was my uncle's only visitor. One day he told me that the staff had dropped him on the floor when giving him a bath. He said that his leg hurt. When I asked the staff they denied that any accident had happened and suggested he was confused. To be honest I felt rather intimidated. Two years later he had some sort of scan done and the report said that there was evidence of an old injury 'possibly a break in the limb'. I felt really guilty for not making more fuss at the time. But I felt even more angry at the apparent 'cover up' by the staff at the home.

It is really important to continue to visit your Cared-for as often as you can even if they suffer from dementia and appear not to be aware of your visit. It is an unfortunate fact that in some homes, those who are visited frequently and have relatives or friends to speak up for them are those who are best cared for. Although it is easy to blame care home staff for this, it is worth remembering that the homes are frequently short-staffed and staff are over-worked and unless someone who visits points out problems to them they may not notice. It is easy, for example, for an overworked care worker to assume that your Cared-for is just not hungry and to remove an uneaten meal when perhaps they actually only needed help in cutting up their food.

The advice above is not supposed to imply that staff in care and nursing homes in general are not kind and caring. But you will know your own Cared-for best and will be able to spot problems and voice the concerns of your friend or relative in the most appropriate manner.

Further information – care and nursing homes

The Elderly Accommodation Counsel
for lists of homes in most areas
www.eac.org.uk
Tel:0207 820 1343

The Registered Nursing Home Association
for a list of registered nursing homes
www.rnha.co.uk
Tel: 0121 454 2511

BUPA Care homes
for a list of general things to look for when choosing a home
www.bupacarehomes.co.uk
Tel: 0800-00-10-10

NHFA (Nursing Home Fees Agency)
The aim of the NHFA is to enable older people to meet the cost of their chosen care whilst also preserving as much of their capital as possible.
www.nhfa.co.uk
Tel:0800-99-88-33

12

Wills and probate

My father-in-law had made a proper will and had left a detailed
inventory of his property and where documents were to be found.
His affairs were in impeccable order and we did not have in this
instance to apply for probate. Even so it took my husband, who
had been appointed executor, several weeks to sort everything
out, and it cost a lot in time, postage and telephone calls. I dread
to think of how difficult it must be for someone dealing with a
less orderly estate.

Many people put off writing a will because it seems morbid or
because death seems so far away. Many are also under the
illusion that if they do not write a will 'my spouse/children will
get everything anyway'. If your relatives, or friends, are under
this impression it is important to disabuse them. If someone dies
without leaving a will ('intestate') then the law has strict criteria
about where the money goes and it may not be where your
relative, or friend, would choose.

It is very likely that the first time you have to consider this
matter is after the death of a relative, perhaps one or other of your

parents, and so this section has been written to give some clear guidance to someone dealing with wills and probate for the first time. Several publications are available which cover the whole subject in more detail and the official probate website is extremely helpful.

Briefly, if your Cared-for has died and left a will the procedure is as follows:

1. Read the will and find out who has been appointed as executor.

2. Inform all the financial institutions involved of the death and of the identity of the executor.

3. Collect details about all bank accounts, stocks and shares, property owned and debts owed to the estate.

4. Collect any details you can find about any debts owed by the person who has died

5. Apply for probate if necessary.

6. After the grant of probate collect funds from all bank and financial accounts, pay debts from this sum and pass the rest to the beneficiaries.

If you are helping to sort out the affairs of an elderly relative, or friend, after the death of their spouse and if the deceased has left a will then this is the easiest scenario. However, 'easy' is a relative term. There are many documents which have to be completed, telephone calls which have to be made and decisions which must be agreed upon. Be prepared for long frustrating waits on the end of a telephone line, difficult discussions and tedious form completion.

The following tips are intended to be helpful and assist you avoiding pitfalls. They are not intended to be a complete guide. It is recommended that you borrow or buy a publication which deals with the subject or download from a website the detailed information for each instance which you might encounter.

Checking the will

Hopefully the deceased will have written a will. A will does not have to be drawn up by a solicitor nor does it have to be complicated to be valid. Your relative or friend may have written their own will, they may have used a 'will form' which can be obtained from a stationer or a website or they may have had a will drawn up by a solicitor. You will need to find the will. Some people lodge the will with a bank or a solicitor for safe-keeping; some people just store it with other important documents in the home. Once you find the document keep it safe. It is worth making some photocopies to work from and perhaps to distribute to other relatives if required. The original will be needed if you have to apply for probate. A will should be signed by the person making it and dated, it should be witnessed by two people who are not beneficiaries and it should appoint an executor. It is likely that your father will have appointed your mother as executor and vice versa in which case the procedure is fairly simple. Sometime people appoint more than one executor. The executor is the person who has the responsibility for 'administering the estate' which means collecting all the credit owed and paying all the debts from the estate and then ensuring that any funds remaining are passed to the beneficiary or beneficiaries. Some people appoint either a solicitor or a bank to be executor of their will and if this is the case you will need to contact the executor institution or professional and they will continue the procedure as below. If you are the carer of an elderly relative or friend and they have been appointed as executor of a will you may have to guide them through the procedures.

Informing those who need to know

Inform all the financial institutions involved of the death and of the identity of the executor. Any accounts/agreements in joint names will need to be changed to the name of the surviving account holder. Most organisations are trained to react quickly and sympathetically to the report of bereavement and many have a dedicated bereavement team to deal with changes to account names and any rebates or reductions in payments. (There is more information on this in Chapter 2.)

At the same time as you deal with these financial matters you could take the opportunity to inform others who need to know. This might include the local library (return library tickets) and relevant social clubs, neighbours and acquaintances, the local hospital if regular outpatients' appointments are kept, the regular caring agency, the hairdresser if appointments are made ahead and so on. The benefit of trying to inform everyone involved is that it saves difficulty later. It can be really upsetting to a surviving partner to receive a reminder from the library about fines due for unreturned books or a friendly call from a fellow church-goer for example and to have to give the news of death all over again. Do not forget items like Satellite TV agreements or Car breakdown agreements. There is often a contract involved with these and the names will have to be changed to keep things valid.

Collect any details you can find about any debts owed by the person who has died. This will include money owing to the Inland Revenue. The Tax Inspector will probably require you to complete a tax return for the portion of the year between the previous April and the death. On receipt of this the Inland Revenue will inform you if any income tax is owing or if a rebate is due. You will need all this information for the Probate application if you are making this. In respect of other debts the executor is responsible for making sure that these have been paid before paying any beneficiaries. There are rules about how to discover debts if you do not know the details. You have to advertise in The London Gazette and in a local paper for anyone who might have a claim on the estate and wait a certain time before paying any beneficiaries. If the estate which you are administering is worth more than a certain amount there will be inheritance tax to pay and you will have to calculate this and pay it to the Inland Revenue before probate is granted.

You do not always have to go through the process of applying for probate. In certain circumstances you can administer the estate and handle all the affairs of the deceased without probate. These circumstances apply when, for example the deceased has left very little money or when everything they had was jointly owned with someone to whom the dead person's share passes automatically (for example, between a married couple) and no building society or bank accounts contain large sums of money. You should check with the probate office if this applies in the case you are dealing with. If you are not applying for probate then, as you contact any financial institutions, explain this straight away. Most institutions have a special form to be completed which enables the account to be transferred into the name of the surviving owner. However, in some cases banks and building societies may insist upon probate being obtained.

My sister and I were named as joint executors. On reading the instructions on the probate form I realised that just one of us could take on the task – the other is allowed to 'opt out' of the administration procedures. However, I was keen for my sister to see that everything was above board and did not suggest this. Later I wished that I had because everything had to be signed by us both. As she lived some distance away this involved a lot of 'to and fro' posting of documents and made everything take longer.

Applying for probate

The term probate means the issuing of a legal document to one or more people authorizing them to administer the estate. The probate registry issues the document, which is called a 'grant of representation'.

These are the three types of grant of representation:

1. Probate: Issued to one or more of the executors named in the deceased's will where executors have been named and are willing to act.

2. Letters of administration (with will): Issued when there is a will, but there is no executor named, or when the executors are unable to apply, or do not wish to be involved in dealing with the estate.

3. Letters of administration: Issued when the deceased had not made a will, or any will made is not valid

If you telephone either the Probate Office or the Inland Revenue and explain the situation they will normally send you a 'Probate Pack' which contains the probate application form (on which you give details of the deceased and the person applying for grant of Probate) and the Account of the estate form which asks you to give a full account of the deceased's estate and also a collection of explanatory notes. Don't be put off by the size of the 'Probate Pack'; it contains forms which you may not have to complete and extensive explanatory notes.

Read through the pack very carefully before you start. Different forms are supplied for different circumstances and it really is easy to begin completing the wrong form and waste a lot of time.

For the Account of Estate form you should try to obtain the full value of all items shown. This means that you should try to get estimates and include any interest or bonus that will be paid to bank or building society accounts. You should also ask share companies about dividends which are due. Any money due from the deceased's employer should be included if your relative died whilst still employed and this may include unpaid salary or a 'death in service' payment. The full market value of any house should be shown, although a professional valuation is not normally required. You can give an informed estimate simply by checking with a local estate agent. The value of household goods, jewellery and belongings should be shown as the amount for which they could be sold and you are generally allowed to make an estimate of this. This form looks extremely complicated but you will probably find that you only have to complete a few parts of it. The explanatory notes are very helpful and usually included in the Probate Pack is a flow chart which helps you to work out what to do at each stage of the procedure. The Probate Office and helpline is also very helpful and telephone queries are answered promptly.

The Probate form asked some very detailed questions about my father-in-law's brothers, sisters, parents and even aunts and uncles! We really didn't know the answers and the explanatory notes didn't help on this question. But when we telephoned the Probate Office they told us that we could just put 'unknown' and the problem was solved. Apparently they would be more likely to need this information if the deceased had died intestate.

As well as ensuring that you collect proper details of the worth of the estate make sure that you keep all details and receipts of any expenses incurred. Certain expenses are allowed to be off-set against the estate before inheritance tax is calculated and you should be sure to do this if you wish to minimise the inheritance tax bill. Some of these allowable expenses are clear such as the funeral director's bill and others are more vague. For example, you can claim miscellaneous 'mourning expenses' which might include the cost of getting to the funeral venue or of purchasing suitable clothing to wear to the funeral. You can claim for the cost of a headstone and for the costs of the refreshments after the funeral.

If you are reading this section in order to deal with the estate of someone who has already died it may be too late to do more than the above in order to minimise inheritance tax but if you are guiding your elderly relative or friend through making a will then it is wise to get proper advice about legal ways to avoid inheritance tax. Many financial institutions and firms of solicitors specialise in this area and a consultation with one of these will be well worth the cost involved.

It may take several weeks or even months to get all the information together and submit the forms. The forms are submitted to the probate office where you wish to go for interview. Most people think they have to go to the office nearest the deceased's home but you can choose the office most convenient for you (and any other executors) to attend. The Probate office will send you a date and time for the interview. The interview is very brief and simply consists of a formal oath that what you have declared is the truth. You can take someone with you to the probate office if you wish but normally you will be interviewed alone.

After the Grant of Probate

After the interview the Grant of Probate is sent to you within a very few days and you can then notify all the financial institutions (and anyone else) and proceed to pay bills and share out the estate.

There was a final share dividend payment which we had to claim and the institution made out a cheque in the names of both my brothers and myself as we were all executors. This made life very difficult as we did not have a joint account and could not pay it into any of our bank accounts. We had to write and ask for the cheque to be made out to just my elder brother (he then shared the money out) but we all had to sign the letter and it caused quite a delay. The bank later told us that we could have opened a joint account for the purposes of administration of the estate.

If there is inheritance tax to pay then probate will not be granted until it is paid. This can appear to be a 'catch 22' situation. If Probate has not been granted how can you obtain the money to pay the inheritance tax? Fortunately many banks and building societies will release money for this purpose from the deceased's account. But they don't always tell you this until you ask!

I was amazed to find out how expensive the funeral costs were. My father had asked for the simplest possible coffin and funeral arrangements but there were some problems. Firstly, other members of the family wanted different arrangements (a better coffin was one demand). I also found that even a 'simple' funeral was not cheap. Fortunately the Funeral Directors explained to me that the bank would release the money from Dad's account to pay for the funeral. I don't think we could have afforded it otherwise.

After probate is granted it is up to the executor to pay any other debts on the estate. If there is not enough money to pay all the debts there is a certain order in which they have to be paid. This order is as follows: first any funeral expenses and expenses involved in dealing with the will, then the Inland Revenue & Customs, any social security debts and any unpaid pension or wages contributions.

Living Wills

'Living wills' are not really wills as such. They are more accurately described as advance directions on stopping life-prolonging treatment. They do not have a legal status and making one does not obviate the need to make a proper will which will come into force upon the death of the person making it. With the advance of medical science there is ever greater potential for individuals to be 'kept alive' without any real prospect of them being able to live for themselves at any time in the future. A living will is supposed to cover the patient's wishes in such a difficult situation. The doctors in charge of your elderly relative or friend do not have to take account of any living will but it sometimes makes the decision-making easier for them and for you.

If your Cared-for would like to make a living will there are a few simple rules that they should follow:

- The document needs to be clear and concise.
- It is helpful if it considers the types of treatment that they would not like to undergo and gives reasons. (This will help others to assess whether they would have consented to a specific treatment.)
- It is worth getting the document witnessed by two people, who, preferably, will not benefit after the death.
- It is also worth consulting the GP.

You can store a living will with an original (after death) will but make sure that it can be accessed easily. Most importantly, your relative or friend needs to make sure that someone (the next of kin) knows of its existence otherwise it may not be acted upon.

Further information – wills and probate

HM Court Service
for advice about Wills and Probate
Tel: 020 7189 2000
www.hmcourts-service.gov.uk/cms/wills.htm

Revenue and Customs
(previously Inland Revenue)
for specific advice about Probate and Inheritance Tax
Tel: 0845 302 0900
www.hmrc.gov.uk/cto/pa1.htm

Community Legal Service
Free leaflets on Wills and Probate
Tel: 0845 345 4345
www.clsdirect.org.uk

Age Concern
Fact sheet on Living Wills
Tel: 020 8765 7200
www.ageconcern.org.uk

Age Concern Scotland
www.ageconcernscotland.org.uk

13

Caring for the carer

Being a carer is very stressful and very tiring. It can also be very fulfilling and many of us are glad to be 'giving something back', especially if it is to a parent who once cared for us. But there is no denying that it can sometimes feel as though we are labouring under an intolerable burden. It is very seldom, even in the best regulated and closest of families, that the burden of caring seems to be shared equally amongst the family members. There may be many reasons for this. Some members of the family may live too far away to give 'hands on' care. Some may have a closer relationship than others with the person being cared for. Some people work longer hours or in more stressful jobs than others. Sometimes, sadly, certain family members do not want to be involved in the care of their relatives. Frequently, the burden of care falls on the family member, or friend if family are not involved, who lives nearest, or who is perceived as having the most time to give. It is a fact that carers are more often female than male and perhaps society sees caring as a female pursuit rather than a male one.

In general it is true to say that the role of 'carer' is not planned for or logically decided upon. In an ideal world, as our relatives or close friends grow steadily more frail, plans would be made for the future, money saved for contingencies, moves made to more manageable accommodation, help enlisted in advance. In the real world people fall ill suddenly, accidents happen, sudden death happens, events overtake us and the role of carer is suddenly ours without planning or forethought.

Very often there is a dramatic change in situation after the death of one member of an elderly partnership. There is a sudden realisation that the remaining partner will not be able to cope alone without substantial input from other members of the family, or friends, 'the carers'. In such an emergency, contingency plans have to be made and actions taken without there being enough time to consider the consequences.

If at all possible time should be made after the initial 'emergency' to take a step back, draw breath and consider a 'care plan'. It is very worthwhile at this stage to get together and agree co-operation with everyone involved. Lack of this co-operation may turn out to be the biggest underlying problem. Resentment and hostility quickly build up in the absence of communication. Guilt plays a part. A daughter living at some distance away may really resent the 'hands on' care given by a daughter-in-law even whilst knowing and understanding that she is unable to give it herself. A son may not feel at all able to give this kind of care and react by belittling the care given by his sisters.

We are a big family and after Dad died it is true to say that each of us took a part in looking after Mum and helping her move house and settle into her new way of life. Looking back we are all able to see that. At the time though, I don't think there was one of us who didn't at some time think that we were the one being put upon and that everyone else was 'slacking'. Some of us were more involved with the practical side of packing up the household and cleaning, others helped sort out the finances and my sister who lived furthest away and couldn't do any day-to-

---

day business took Mum away to stay with her for the weekend on several occasions. It's only looking back that we can all see the part each of us played. At the time, shock and guilt really did interfere with clear thinking. If we hadn't been such a close family I believe we could have fallen out permanently then.

Group meetings early on, where concrete plans are made and (if possible) where recriminations are withheld will help avoid such situations developing. If someone lives too far away to help with daily care, perhaps they can agree to come and stay at intervals and give 'holiday cover' to the chief carer. Someone who is not good at practical personal care may instead be able to manage the financial affairs. It helps to make use of personal strengths here. Someone who enjoys cooking may agree to keep the Cared-for's freezer stocked with ready meals whilst someone who is only free once a week but is a car driver might organise the shopping. A family member who works within the health service may act as the co-ordinator for healthcare.

There is no reason why, once the initial emergency is over, the family and friends should not hold their own regular assessments of what needs to be done and draw up their own 'care plan' at intervals. If possible, do not let the plethora of tasks which need to be done build up in a piecemeal fashion. Care needs are likely to be constantly changing. Gradually you may find that the level of care needs to be increased or changed to suit a changing state of health or disability in your relative or friend. Sometimes care needs may decrease - for example, following recuperation after a hospital admission.

There were five of us involved in caring for Mum and at first we found we were all so busy that we never found time to meet and discuss what each of us was doing. Sometimes we found we had 'doubled up' on things and other things slipped through the net because we weren't communicating. One Christmas after a family get together we made a decision to meet up again in three months to discuss how things were going and whether we needed to make other changes. This quarterly get-together became a family reunion and we kept it up even after Mum died. We still start the day with a toast to Mum because without her we might have all drifted apart more.

What if you are the only family member? You should not try to take on everything alone. There may well be neighbours or friends of your Cared-for who will help in the same way that family do. Otherwise you will have to turn to professional help. There is no need to feel guilt over this. Indeed some elderly people prefer the notion that any help they are receiving is 'paid' help and not done as a favour. Remember that you do not have to go through social services to get professional help, although you may wish to do so (see Chapter 10 on Care agencies and professional carers).

Caring for a member of the family is an unpaid 'occupation' but you or your Cared-for may be able to claim certain grants and allowances (see Chapter 3 Financial Matters, page 45 Benefits) and if you are entitled to them you should certainly claim them. Do not allow your Cared-for, or yourself, to be put off by thoughts of 'living off the state' or claiming 'charity'. Most of us have paid into the state through National Insurance contributions and all of us are entitled to claim help from the state when we need it. There is an additional factor. Being in receipt of certain benefits often qualifies you for other financial help or gives you priority when seeking other 'non cash' benefits. Some benefits are means tested and the entitlement may in itself mean very little. You may think that the receipt of say forty pence per week is not worth the effort of claiming *but* the extra benefits may make it very worth while. An example of this is Disability Living Allowance. If your

Cared-for is in receipt of this allowance at the higher rate they automatically qualify for a 'blue badge', which allows parking in 'disabled' car park spaces. Being in receipt of Incapacity Benefit may entitle one to help with Council tax payments.

Conversely, receipt of certain benefits may make you or the person you care for ineligible for other benefits which might be more useful to you both or make you financially better off. The whole benefits area is a bit of a minefield and it can be helpful to take advice from one of the organisations that specialise in giving information in this area. There are some websites which enable you to check out your eligibility (see Further Information, page 220) or you can contact the Department of Work and Pensions benefits helpline or talk to an adviser at the Citizens' Advice Bureau.

You may not realise that if you are a carer, you can ask the local authority for an assessment of your own needs. If you live in England or Wales you are entitled to an assessment whether or not the person you are caring for is having an assessment themselves. In Scotland you can only receive an assessment if the person you are caring for is being assessed. Except in Scotland, where there is no standard list of what should be assessed, the assessment is supposed to take into account your work or desire to work and your need for training, education and leisure activities. The kind of help and support you can get as a carer includes: respite care to give you a break if you are caring constantly for your relative; emotional support from other carers usually through a local support group, help with caring, and help with household tasks and activities for the person you care for. You should also be told about any benefits you are entitled to claim. Your assessment may be made by a social worker from the local authority social services department or it may be carried out by a worker from a private agency employed on behalf of social services.

Before you have an assessment you might want to think about the following because these are things that you may be asked about and will perhaps need to write notes on:

- If you need to get up in the night to care for your relative or friend are you getting enough sleep?
- Are you able to get out and do things by yourself or does your Cared-for need to have someone with them constantly?
- Do you feel that your health is being affected by caring? For example, are you having to do any heavy lifting (physical health) or is the situation making you depressed (mental health)?
- Are you able to cope with other family commitments? Are you also having to run a home and care for husband/wife and children?
- Are you finding juggling work and caring difficult? You may have to work to earn a living and are having to fit caring in around your working day.

Talk to the person doing your assessment about these and any other issues that you think may affect your ability to continue caring. Remember that by caring for your relative or friend you are helping to maintain the current state policy of ensuring 'care in the community' and are saving the state money in terms of possible care home fees.

If you feel that you need an urgent assessment (if you suddenly have to go into hospital, for example) then make this clear to the social services Duty Officer because they are able to organise 'emergency assessments'. (See also the notes on **intermediate care** in Chapter 10, page 174.)

In a perfect world we would receive all the help needed to care for our relative or friend through official channels and all the facilities would be there to assist us. In actual fact the level of help available varies widely from area to area. Local authorities have limited resources and have to give the help they can to those most in need based on their own assessment of where the need is greatest. So it is fairly certain that you will have to find ways and means to relieve some of the burden of caring for yourself.

First, do not neglect to ask for help from your Cared-for's friends and neighbours if you need it. Carers are a huge 'silent force' within the community and many struggle on feeling that to ask for help is a confession of weakness and inability to cope. As well as using the services of the local authority, actively seek for other informal help. Friends and neighbours may well be able and willing to fill 'gaps' in the help supplied officially. Many people are pleased and even flattered to be asked to help but the most important advice here is to be specific. A neighbour will often promise to 'keep an eye on things' but it would be much more useful if you asked them to do something specific - say, 'Can you call round each morning just to check all is well?' or 'Could you pick up and change the library books on Thursdays?' Of course, people may sometimes be unable to help but unless and until you ask you will never know.

One of the ladies at our local church suffered from vascular dementia. Her husband was quite dedicated and refused to allow her to go into a nursing home, continuing to look after her himself until just a few weeks before she died. A group of parishioners from the 'Senior Citizens Group' got together and formed a rota to sit with the poor lady once a week so that her husband could have a few hours to himself. Sometimes he went visiting or had an outing and sometimes he just caught up on some sleep. He had some respite and she had the company of people she knew. He told me afterwards that he would not have been able to cope without this respite and because it was done on a rota basis no one person felt they had to take on too much.

Also investigate local clubs and organisations to which your Cared-for belongs. If they belong to a church you will almost certainly be able to get help to transport them to church services and perhaps a lift to any church related clubs they belong to or you might get respite in the form of visitors or help with shopping and other errands. If your Cared-for belongs to a local branch of an organisation such as The British Legion (for example) ask if members can offer any help. Ex-service men and women's organisations can be particularly helpful and many elderly people are ex-service people due to war service and National Service in the years that followed the Second World War. Another alternative source of help can be local branches of organisations set up to benefit ex-members of professions or trades. Some examples are given in the chapter references, but if you can't find the appropriate organisation there keep investigating. Use the local library or the internet as a starting point.

Local and national charities can also be sources of help. You may think that your needs or those of your Cared-for are too insignificant to be of interest to these charities but you may be surprised to learn that some charities, far from having their resources stretched too thinly, are desperate to find those who need their help.

My friend was temporary Chief Executive of a charity which gave help to those who could not afford to pay their water charges. He surprised me by telling me one day that the charity had great trouble finding people who they could help, not because the help was not needed but because their advertising was poor and that therefore those who needed their help were not being informed that it was available for the asking.

If you feel you need it, make sure you also organise support for yourself. There are several organisations aimed at supporting carers (see Further Information, page 220). Some of these offer information, some offer practical support and some offer 'moral support' in the form of local support groups where carers can meet to talk about their problems or concerns with people who are in a similar situation to them. There are often separate groups which give support to carers of those suffering from dementia. Your local GP surgery will almost certainly have information about local support groups or you can ask the district nursing team about them. Information about national carers' organisations can be obtained from the internet or from your local library.

It can be difficult, but try not to allow yourself to feel constantly guilty. Those who we care for do not always show their appreciation, and indeed in some cases, they may be unable to do so. Parents have grown used to nagging their children, old friends have grown used to taking help given for granted. Other members of the family may find it easier to find fault with the care you are giving rather than offer support. Try always to assure yourself that you are doing the best you can. Do not feel guilty if you sometimes feel annoyed with or speak crossly to those you care for. If you feel that your feelings may get the better of you and lead to any form of action stronger than cross words make every attempt to stand back from the situation and seek help.

It is most important that the carer considers their own health and sanity as well as that of their Cared-for. You should never neglect your own health issues because if you are ill your Cared-for will suffer as well since you will be unable to give the level of care you would wish to.

A friend of mine, in his 80s himself, was looking after his wife with Alzheimer's syndrome and refused to leave her for any length of time. He got so exhausted that he slipped down the stairs and knocked himself out, with loss of memory afterwards. After such a head injury he should have been observed in hospital for signs of bleeding inside his skull but, because of his sense of duty, he refused to be admitted. Three weeks later he had a fit and was admitted with a large blood clot on the brain and continuing bleeding. He later died and his wife had to be admitted to a residential home - the very thing he had, mistakenly, been trying to avoid.

If you visit your doctor for a health problem which needs a referral to an outpatient clinic or involves being referred for an operation, make sure that the doctor knows you are a carer. When referring patients, doctors take into account not only the severity of the health problem referred but also any circumstances in the patient's life that might mean they should be seen more quickly than normal. This is standard practice but your doctor cannot take the fact that you are a carer into account if he does not know that you are. These days most doctors do not know their patients personally and, although they should ask you about problems of everyday living which might be affecting your health, many do not have time to do so. So tell the doctor that you are a carer for your relative, or friend, and if you are going to have to make special arrangements for their care in order to get treatment for your own health make sure that the doctor knows this.

If you are a full-time carer you should do your very best to build in some 'respite' time. You might pay for a carer to come in and sit with your Cared-for once or twice a week or you might be able to find a friend, neighbour or other family member who will do this. You may find a local charity or other organisation who will provide this service. If you are regularly woken at night in order to care for your relative or friend, then for your own safety you should try to organise at least one night of unbroken sleep each week. There are agencies which provide a 'night sitting' service or you could ask another member of the family to give you relief from night duty on a regular basis.

Even if you are not caring for your relative or friend full time you will want to go away on holiday occasionally. Another member of the family, or a friend or neighbour may be prepared to take over your visiting and caring duties for the length of the holiday. The fact is that families can sometimes be quite selfish over this and so you may have to be prepared to be insistent. An alternative option is to try to arrange respite care for your relative or friend in a local care or nursing home. There can be certain difficulties over this. Although theoretically most homes offer this facility, your chosen home may not have room at the time you need it. The other possibility is that your Cared-for may be quite stubborn about going away for respite care. They may be worried that it is 'the thin end of the wedge' and is leading up to a permanent placement in a care home, which they may dread. They may just not want to leave their familiar surroundings. Familiarity is an important element of independence for the elderly, particularly for those with any form of disability such as poor sight or difficulty in getting about around the house. If this is the case, try to enlist the help of other family members to persuade your Cared-for that you need the break (see Chapter 1 on Managing change). Don't forget that the local authority social services department have a 'duty of care' for carers as well as those cared for so if you can't make informal arrangements or can't find a local Care/Nursing home to help, contact the Duty Officer in the social services department.

Make use of all the resources you can to help your Cared-for and yourself. Read books, check magazine articles, ask at the library, search the internet. Buy or arrange provision of any equipment that will make life easier. Above all, ask what is available. Especially ask your district nursing team. They have access to a lot of information and contacts.

I was nagging my teenage son one day about some task that he hadn't done and he responded wittily with, ' Careful Dad, I'll be the one choosing your nursing home when the time comes!' It was meant as a joke of course, but it did make me start to take stock of what future I wanted for myself.

At this point it occurs to many carers to think about their own future. Many of us have plans for our retirement but for most of us, in our imagination and planning this means 'active retirement'. It is very difficult to think about planning for a frail old age because most of us do not want to imagine this future. However, if you don't want to be in the position of having others make decisions for you, then make your plans now for this possible future. It is a very good time to make plans whilst you are caring for another because the difficulties and limitations of frail old age will be clearly before you (as well, perhaps, as the compensations). So, this could be an ideal time to think about the following:

- Where would you like to live and what would be the most practical accommodation? Many people have a vision of old age in a bungalow, which is why bungalows are so highly sought after. However, with modern facilities such as lifts then a small flat might be the answer. Many 'retirement' complexes are being designed and built now to cater for the aging population and if you have the chance you could look around some and decide what is likely to suit you when the time comes.

> We were so lucky in finding Mum a house in a 'mixed' complex. There were several small privately owned cottages, each designed for one or two elderly people and a small block of rented flats all owned by the same Trust. There was a resident warden and a social centre and the communal gardens were all beautifully maintained. She retained her sense of independence because the house was hers but she was able to use the social facilities and had company nearby when she wanted it. However, we had quite a search to find just the right place for her and she had to go on the waiting list for several months before one of the houses came up for sale.

- Do you have small physical problems now (arthritis, for example) which might develop in the future and mean that you would need special aids and equipment to manage to be independent? Now is the time to look at catalogues and keep an eye on new developments in the equipment field. Now is the time to put aside money if you think expensive items of aid equipment might be needed.
- Plan for your pension. Most of us realise that the state pension is not going to be enough to live on. Personal pension planning needs to begin many years before we need it. Think ahead about nursing home fees in case they might be required. There are special plans available which mean that you can make allowances for nursing home fess whilst still maintaining as much of your capital as possible. (See Further Information on page 220 and Chapter 3 on finance.)
- Make a will. Many people believe that if they do not make a will their next of kin will automatically get all their estate. This does not happen. See Chapter 12 on wills and probate.
- Think about arranging Power of Attorney in case you need it. It doesn't have to be implemented until you want to but it has to be drawn up whilst you are able to understand what you are doing and can sign the documents. Do not be put off. This does not only mean thinking in terms of dementia but considering what would be the needs of your family if, for example, you suffered a stroke and could not sign cheques or use your debit card.
- Why not spend time getting to know about the kinds of care homes and nursing homes available and even look at one or two just in case. If in the future you need this level of care why let others decide for you then when you can make your own decisions now.
- Write down your wishes for the future. Discuss them with

your next of kin, your family and your friends. Don't let people tell you that you are being morbid. Explain that it will make their lives easier if they know what you want to happen if you get very frail.

* Don't get depressed by all this forward thinking. Feel secure in that you have made all the plans you possibly can.

Further information – caring for the carer

Counsel and Care
Information for the elderly and for carers
www.counselandcare.org.uk
Tel: 020 7241 8555

Carers UK
(links to sites for Scotland, Wales and Northern Ireland)
Tel: 0207 490 8818
www.carersuk.org

The Princess Royal Trust for Carers
Tel: London Office: 020 7480 7788 /
Glasgow Office: 0141 221 5066
www.carers.org

Civil Service Retirement Fellowship
The Civil Service Retirement Fellowship exists to help retired civil servants (home visits, local newsletters and group social events). Both retired and serving civil servants can join the Fellowship.
Tel:020 8691 7411
www.crsf.org.uk

Soldiers, Sailors, Airmen and Families Association (SSAFA). National charity helping serving and ex-Service men, women and their families, including widows and widowers in need.
Tel: 0845 1300 975
www.ssafa.org.uk

The Royal British Legion
Provides financial, social and emotional support to those who have served and are currently serving in the Armed Forces, and their dependants
Telephone +44 (0)8457 725 725
www.britishlegion.org.uk

Nursing Home Fees Agency
Gives advice on funding Nursing Home Fees
Tel: 01865 733000
www.nhfa.co.uk

Benefits Now
This site enables you to assess yourself for Disability Living Allowance or Attendance allowance before you apply. You can find out whether you qualify and at what rate you are likely to be paid
www.benefitsnow.co.uk

Useful contacts

Age Concern England
Tel: 020 8765 7200
www.ageconcern.org.uk

Age Concern Scotland
Tel: 0800 009966
www.ageconcernscotland.org.uk

Alzheimer's Society
UK's leading care and research charity for people with dementia, their families
and carers
Tel: 020 7306 0606
www.alzheimers.org.uk

Alzheimer Scotland
Tel: 0808 808 3000 (helpline)
www.alzscot.org

Carers UK
The leading campaigning, policy and information organisation for carers
(links to sites for Scotland, Wales and Northern Ireland)
Tel: 0207 490 8818
www.carersuk.org

Civil Service Retirement Fellowship
The Civil Service Retirement Fellowship exists to help retired civil
servants (home visits, local newsletters and group social events). Both retired
and serving civil servants can join.
Tel:020 8691 7411
www.crsf.org.uk

Counsel and Care
Information for the elderly and for carers
Tel: 020 7241 8555
www.counselandcare.org.uk

Crossroads – caring for carers
Provides trained and qualified carers to give respite care
Tel: 0845 4500350 (helpline)
www.crossroads.org.uk

Department for Transport
General information about transport facilities for the elderly
www.dft.gov.uk
Information about the Blue Badge scheme
www.direct.gov.uk/DisabledPeople

for dementia
Seeks to improve the quality of life for people affected by dementia.
Tel: 020 7874 7210
www.fordementia.org.uk

Foundations
Information on local Home Improvement Agencies to help older
people stay in their own homes
Tel: 01457 891909
www.foundations.uk.com

Help The Aged
Tel: 0808 800 6565 (senior advice line)
www.helptheaged.org.uk

Macmillan Cancer Relief
Tel: 0808 808 2020 (helpline)
www.macmillan.org.uk

Multiple Sclerosis Society
Tel: 0808 800 8000 (helpline)
www.mssociety.org.uk

Princess Royal Trust for Carers
The largest provider of comprehensive Carers' support services in the UK. Through
its unique network of independently managed Carers' Centres, young carers'
services and interactive websites (www.carers.org; www.youngcarers.net), The

Trust provides quality information, advice and support services to carers of all ages.
Tel: London Office: 020 7480 7788 / Glasgow Office: 0141 221 5066
www.carers.org

Rethink
Helping everyone affected by severe mental illness to recover a better quality of life.
Tel: 0845 456 0455
www.rethink.org

Royal British Legion
Provides financial, social and emotional support to those who have served and are currently serving in the Armed Forces, and their dependants.
Telephone +44 (0)8457 725 725
www.britishlegion.org.uk

Soldiers, Sailors, Airmen and Families Association (SSAFA).
National charity helping serving and ex-Service men, women and their families, including widows and widowers in need.
Tel: 0845 1300 975
www.ssafa.org.uk

Equipment and Aids

Disabled Living Foundation
Provides information and advice on equipment. There is an Equipment Demonstration Centre with large displays of equipment which visitors can try out and where advice can be obtained.
Helpline: 0845 130 9177 (charged at Local Call Rate)
Equipment Demonstration Centre: (020) 7289 6111 ext.247
www.dlf.org.uk

Assist UK Disabled Living Centres
A network of centres around the UK which provides information and advice on products and where you can see and try our products.
Tel: 0870 770 2866
www.dlcc.org.uk

British Red Cross
Ability Catalogue - products for Independence
Tel: 0870 739 7391
www.redcross.org.uk

Incontinence Products
Tel: 0800 180 4325
www.dryforlife.co.uk

Keep Able
Mobility and lifestyle ideas, with nationwide chain of shops plus an online store.
Tel: 08705 202122
www.keepable.co.uk

Lloydspharmacy
Local pharmacy branches stock catalogues of aids and equipment and can order items for you and have them delivered to your nearest pharmacy. The website has a 'nearest pharmacy' search facility.
www.lloydspharmacy.co.uk

BenefitsNow On-line shop
For elastic shoe laces and other aids for living
www.benefitsnowshop.co.uk

Gimble
Hands free reading device
www.gimbleuk.com

RNIB
Royal National Institute for the Blind
Tel: 0845 702 3153
www.onlineshop.rnib.org.uk

RNID
Royal National Institute for Deaf People
Tel: 0870 789 8855
www.rnidshop.com

Royal Association for Disability and Rehabilitation (RADAR)
Tel: 020 7250 3222
www.radar.org.uk

Stair-lifts

Stannah
Tel: 0800 715 171
www.stannah.com

Brooks Stairlifts
Tel: 0800 834730
www.stairlifts.co.uk

Walking Aids

Uniscan Walkers
Tel: 0800 0640762
www.uniscan-walkers.co.uk

Able Mail Order
Tel:0800 358 0445
www.independentliving.co.uk/able/mailorder.html

Financial

Benefits Now
This site enables you to assess yourself for Disability Living Allowance or
Attendance allowance before you apply. You can find out whether you qualify
and at what rate you are likely to be paid.
www.benefitsnow.co.uk

Nursing Home Fees Agency
Specialist care fee advisers.
Tel: 01865 733000
www.nhfa.co.uk

Public Guardianship Office
Information about Power of Attorney.
0845 330 2900
www.guardianship.gov.uk

Citizen's advice Bureau
The Citizens Advice service helps people resolve their legal, financial and other
problems by providing free, independent and confidential advice.
Local telephone numbers
www.citizensadvice.org.uk

Department of Work and Pensions Benefit Enquiry Line
Confidential advice and information for people with disabilities, and their car-
ers and representatives, about social security benefits and how to claim them.
Phone: 0800 88 22 00 (Free)

Health and nutrition

WRVS
Voluntary organisation working to support people in need who might otherwise feel lonely and isolated, at home, in hospital or at times of crisis.
Tel: 01235 442900
www.wrvs.org.uk

The Outside Clinic
Offers eye tests and an eye care service in your own home.
Tel: 0500 295 245
www.outsideclinic.com

Social

Independent Occupational Therapy
Occupational Therapists in Independent Practice
Tel: 0800 389 4873
www.otip.co.uk

The Elderly Accommodation Counsel
For lists of homes in most areas.
Tel: (020) 7820 1343
www.eac.org.uk

Commission for Social Care Inspection
The single, independent inspectorate for all social care services in England, working on a local and national level. The website includes lists of care homes by region, with maps, and inspection reports.
Tel: 0845 015 0120
www.csci.org.uk

The Registered Nursing Home Association
For a list of registered nursing homes.
Tel: 0121 454 2511
www.rnha.co.uk

BUPA Care homes
For a list of general things to look for when choosing a home.
Tel: 0800 00 1010
www.bupacarehomes.co.uk

Contact for the Elderly
Sunday afternoon tea for lonely people (restricted areas)
Tel: 0800 716543

Cruse Bereavement Care
Help, Counselling and support for the bereaved.
Tel: 0870 167 1677 (helpline)
www.crusebereavementwcare.org.uk

Boogaloo
Craft kits and hobby materials.
Tel: 0870 787 7082
www.Boogaloo.co.uk

Royal National Institute for the Blind
Talking books and other products for the blind and partially sighted.
Tel: 0845 762 6843
www.rnib.co.uk

Royal National Institute for the Deaf
Online shop with aids for every day living for the deaf.
Tel: 0870 789 8855
Textphone: 01733 238020
www.rnid.org.uk

Windsor Products
Books on 'Computing made easy' and freebies for older folk.
Tel: 0870 050 7791
www.windsorproducts.com

Gardening for Disabled Trust
The Trust gives grants to people all over the United Kingdom in order that they
may continue to garden, despite advancing illness, age or disability.
Contact: The Secretary
Gardening for Disabled Trust
Hayes Farmhouse
Hayes Lane
Peasmarsh, Rye
East Sussex TN31 6XR

Index